Plot fiction like the Masters: Ian Fleming, Jane Austen, Evelyn Waugh and the Secrets of Story-building

by

Terry Richard Bazes

Copyright © 2015 by Terry Richard Bazes

All rights reserved. No part of this book may be reproduced or transmitted in any form or by any means, without the written permission of the author, except by a reviewer who may quote brief passages in a review.

Registered with the Library of Congress.
Library of Congress subject heading:
   1. Plots (Drama, novel etc.) 2. Fiction – Technique.

Cover Design by Derek Murphy.
Front cover image: *The Distrest Poet*, William Hogarth c.1736, oil on canvas, 65.9 cm x 79.1 cm
Back Cover Image by Louis Netter
ISBN: 978-0-692-39956-9

ROSENCRANTZ & GUILDENSTERN PUBLISHERS

"Why, man, they did make love to this employment."
-- *Hamlet*, Act V, scene ii

Table of Contents

Foreword
Introduction
The Case of James Bond
Pride, Prejudice and Plot-making
Waugh and the Architecture of Dark Comedy
Conflict and the Logic of Story-building
About the Author

Foreword

If many of the other How-To-Write-A-Book books were entitled *How Not To Write A Book*, we'd have a better world and better books as well.

When I was a child, someone gave me a kit that made it possible for anyone to create a masterpiece. Along with some paints and brushes, the kit included a canvas divided into numbered sections of various sizes and shapes. You were to paint each numbered section with a different paint (1 for red, 2 for blue, 3 for chartreuse etc.). Once this mechanical process had been completed, the artist would have produced the Mona Lisa. Only not quite.

Romance novels are big business, but you don't have to read in order to fall in love, and most of us do fall in love. Sometimes we discover that our little adventure is tragic, sometimes just the prelude to a long and bitter association. No matter the final outcome, none but a cold-hearted cad would plot out the romance beforehand. There isn't a formula for falling in love. You simply fall in love.

Terry Bazes is one of those men who has fallen in love with books. He's written two splendid novels. Before that, he earned a PhD in Literature and this was done when the study of literature was still an act of love. Men and women got PhD's in literature, because they loved books and not because they weren't practical enough for engineering.

In this excellent little book Terry Bazes takes a look at three other books, books he has loved, books he still loves. He doesn't butcher them, doesn't hurt them at all, but follows these books around with a notebook and binoculars. He looks for the qualities that many great novels have in common.

He talks about structure, but he never forgets that it is not the design of a book that makes it great. Great books, like all people, have one feature in common -- and that one feature is that they are alive.

Terry Bazes' observations are helpful, sometimes brilliant. He knows how books live, and his astute insights can help bring your book to life. But if you want to write a book that's any good, the first place you need to look is inside. Writing a book is not the same as solving an equation. Books don't solve the world: they enliven it.

In order to write a book that's even decent, you must make use of the world you already have, the world that you come from, the world that you are. Disappointing? Yes. Shameful? Of course.

That's the bad news. The good news is that we all have stories inside us. We all have enough different characters in our head to field a baseball team.

You don't want to die with those people inside you. Nurture them and let them out. Sometimes they'll fall in love. Sometimes they'll fall in hate. Sometimes they'll kill one another. It's heartbreaking to see your own offspring die. But if you mean to write a book, then you will have to break your heart.

Benjamin Cheever

Introduction

"Nor is there singing school but studying monuments of its own magnificence."
-- William Butler Yeats, *Sailing to Byzantium*

This book is an exercise in reading like a writer – reading with the purpose of figuring out how the plots of a few recognized masterpieces succeed in making readers turn the page. The reason for proposing this as a way of learning plot-making is my own experience as a writer -- that the most accomplished novelists are the greatest teachers and that their lessons may be drawn from a close study of their work. So this little book is, in its own way, an application of the scientific method . . . except that the facts under scrutiny are not the conjugal habits of marmosets but the living plots of three justly – and lavishly -- celebrated novels. For these three novels – Ian Fleming's *Dr. No*, Jane Austen's *Pride and Prejudice* and Evelyn Waugh's *A Handful of Dust* – have all achieved astonishing success. They are all not only recognized masterpieces of their very different genres but have also won the glittering prizes – fame, fortune, movie deals -- for which many a haggard writer would sell his or her soul to the Devil.

Ever since Aristotle there have been many names for the steps of a story. And the jargon only matters if it *helps us to understand how a good plot works -- and how to make one.* Many books have been written, terms coined and diagrams drawn to elucidate the mysteries of plot construction. One of the most useful diagrams, included in his *Technique of the Drama* (1863), was Gustave Freytag's famous pyramid.

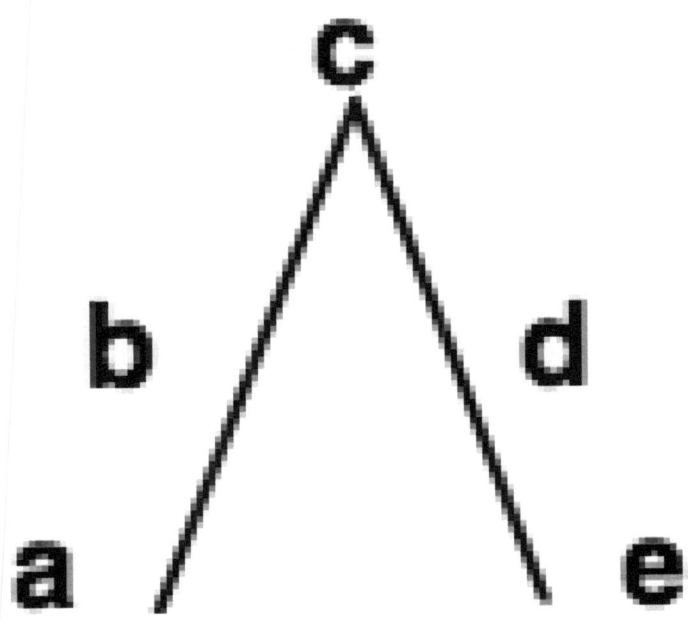

Because Freytag saw that the "two halves of" of a dramatic "action . . . come closely together at one point," he suggested that a drama is shaped like a pyramid. Accordingly, he divided his story pyramid into five component parts: (a) the introduction, (b) the rise, (c) the climax, (d) the fall and (f) the catastrophe. In addition to these five parts, Freytag also gave his pyramid three steps (or "dramatic moments") – only one of which he declared to be "necessary to every play." He called this "necessary" step the "exciting moment" – and placed it on his pyramid in between (a) the introduction and (b) the rise.

    Ever since Herr Freytag posited his six essential and two optional steps needed for climbing up and down his dramatic pyramid, books about story construction have varied in the number of the "plot points" necessary to create absorbing fiction. The magic number has been as few as five, sometimes seven and sometimes more than twenty. Sometimes it is said that they should be designed to fit into a three-act structure – and sometimes not.

    A whole host of terms have also been employed to explain the craft of story building – motivation, backstory, goal, spine, conflict, revelation etc. All of these plotting terms (including Freytag's pyramid) can be extremely useful – even essential. But unless theories are informed by the specifics of successful stories, they are (for me, at least) of limited value. And so it is most helpful to make use of this terminology only in response to the particulars of plotting embedded in their living context. That is why this book is not about how plots *should* be made – but how, in three extraordinary novels, they actually *were* made.

    Putting aside the pyramid metaphor for a moment, one might say that a great plot is a page-turning machine. The reader is immediately grabbed by it and then pulled along by an ever-changing, propulsive dynamic of suspense, curiosity and surprise. All three of these very different novels -- a James Bond thriller, a prototypical "Regency Romance" and a scathing 20th-century black comedy – are driven forward by this kind of engine. One of the chief objectives of this book is not only to examine the parts of this engine as it moves along, but also to discover the secret of the energy that propels it forward. Another objective, when possible, is to look for clues that might suggest how these engines (or pyramids) were built. For it is one thing to look at a pyramid or at a roller coaster – and quite another thing to build one. And that is what the novelist must do.

The Case of James Bond

"The protagonist and the antagonist must be dangerous foes to each other. Both of them are ruthless."
                    Lajos Egri, *The Art of Dramatic Writing*

One of the truisms repeated again and again in books about plotting is that the main character must change. At the end of the fiction, it is said, he must be different than he was at the beginning. The knight – male or female – must have been transformed by his or her quest. This truism, as far as it goes, is quite true. Hamlet, Tom Jones, Emma Bovary, Pip in *Great Expectations*, the narrator is Joyce's *Araby*: all are different at the end of their stories than they were when we first met them. But this cannot be said of James Bond.

And yet the James Bond opus (whatever else can be said about it) is a collection of very good stories. The question, for those of us who undertake to write fiction, is why this so. The question is an important one because, if we can answer it, we just might be able to find the magic key that will enable us unlock the treasure chest inside ourselves that holds the stories of our own.

Ian Fleming, like many novelists, seems to have been recurrently rewriting the same book. The same stock characters and dramatic situations are modified and recycled in each new story. His world-famous repertory company consists of three main players – Bond, the super-villain and the beautiful girl. It also includes a supporting cast whose parts are adapted to each new adventure – not only M and Money Penny, but also the sometimes doomed buddy figure. But for the purposes of the writer who is studying the art of plotting, it is Bond and the super-villain who are most worthy of respectful attention. For they afford a prime example of how the conflict of adversaries – even without truly changing the protagonist – can create an absorbing plot.

One of the well-known axioms of plot construction is that the story must begin with a crucial event (Freytag's "exciting moment") that triggers the drama by sending the hero on his quest. The first chapter of *Dr. No* is a masterful example of such an incident. It is composed of two related murders: first, the murder of Strangways, the spy chief, by three supposed blind men; and then the second murder, of Mary Trueblood, Strangways' female assistant. The triggering event concludes when the murderers set fire to the station and throw the bodies in a reservoir. Not the least impressive aspect of this incident is its economy: these two acts of sadistic violence are precisely rendered in only six pages.

The story has begun so dramatically and so artfully that the casual reader might take it for granted that the conflict of adversaries has already begun. But that is just exactly what we, as writers, cannot afford to overlook. The important fact to keep in mind is that Fleming constructed his plot with this conflict as its center. He has set up a chessboard of opposing forces – and now black has made its first move. And yet there is even more to this triggering event that we writers mustn't miss: Fleming has withheld both the identity and the motive of the three blind men who committed the murders. So he has not only triggered a conflict, but also created a mystery.

It is only now that James Bond walks onstage. While the triggering incident in the opening chapter belongs to the black pieces on the chessboard, the second chapter belongs to the white ones. Another of the time-honored dictums of plot construction is that, at the moment that the trigger propels him into motion, the protagonist should be in the "status quo situation" -- in the routine of everyday life. When we now see Bond – walking into M's office on a wintry March day – he fits this requirement exactly. After a "dreary convalescence" from the poison Rosa Klebb stabbed into his calf at the end of *From Russia with Love*, he is now sitting opposite M – "the symbol of normality he had longed for." He is, in other words, at home base, when M gives him the supposed "holiday task" of investigating the apparently romantic disappearance of Strangways and Mary Trueblood. It is this assignment that sends Bond on his quest, and so the opening sequence of the plot – black's move countered by white's – is complete.

Fleming seems to have constructed this second chapter with two main objectives in mind: providing Bond's motivation and promising the reader future conflict. He planned to accomplish his first objective by having the scene in M's office build to its turning point -- to the crucial moment when Bond accepts the mission that will now create the so-called "spine" of the story. This essential plot point (that also might be thought of as the beginning of the climb up Freytag's pyramid) takes place in a sentence so brief and seemingly artless that a casual reader might miss it: "Bond reached across and picked up the file." By the Bond time has done this – picked up his file and embarked on his mission, Fleming has also already accomplished his second objective. For by now M has told Bond all about the mysterious deaths on Crab Key – providing details (like the man who was burned to death by a fire-breathing dragon) that whet the reader's appetite for future scenes of violence.

 The casual reader, having been hooked by this opening action and reaction-- the triggering event and the counterbalancing outset of the hero's quest -- will now follow Bond to Jamaica, the first stop on his travels before he ventures to the island owned by Dr. No. But we are not casual readers – far from it. Instead, we are readers who are writers – who read not only for enjoyment, but also in order to figure out how books are made. And that's why we're not (at least not yet) going to focus on Bond's arrival in Jamaica – at the way Fleming designed the escalation of the conflict and the introduction of the romantic subplot.
 Instead let's skip ahead to the end of Fleming's plot, to the final battle between the opposing forces he introduced at its beginning. For another of the oft-repeated tenets of plot construction is that the triggering event releases forces that will reach a climax at a dramatic apex known as the "obligatory scene." Think of it (putting aside our chess metaphor for the time being) as an arrow being released from a bow and aiming straight for the bulls-eye of a target. The triggering incident and

the obligatory scene – the release of the bowstring and the target – cannot be thought of independently of one another. Instead, they are two complementary and interdependent components of one dynamic action.

The obligatory scene (the crisis) in *Dr. No* is Bond's life-or-death encounter with the giant squid. The chapter that immediately precedes it is devoted to the increasingly hideous tortures to which Bond is subjected while crawling through a tunnel in Dr. No's mountain fortress. But the giant tarantulas and burning metal walls of the tunnel are only Dr. No's sadistic preliminaries to his *coup de grace.* This battle with the squid is the decisive moment of Bond's greatest vulnerability, pain and horror – and the final confrontation between the opposing forces introduced by the black and white countermoves of the opening chapters. This crucial scene is, in other words, the moment of truth, the showdown – what we've been waiting for.

The major point for us as plot-builders to take away is that an obligatory scene like this one – although it belongs near the end of the dramatic action – should be planned (or at least roughed in) early on. Because this scene is the confrontation, the crisis, that the triggering event anticipates, these two interrelated mechanisms of the plot should be designed simultaneously.

If a writer does this – doesn't only conceive of a triggering event but also sketches a crisis at the very beginning of the plot-building process – he or she can avoid a lot of unnecessary grief. For the danger in ignoring this strategy – in only creating a dramatic opening and in trusting that an ending will somehow fortuitously occur to you – is that you may soon find yourself wandering in a maze of aimless incidents. But if you also start out with an ending in view – and, so to speak, write backwards – you won't lose your way at the beginning.

Of course the design of the obligatory scene (in this instance Bond's battle with the squid) depends upon the nature of the adversaries – who always function as the principal players in any plot although they put on different masks for different kinds of stories. In a mystery story they are the detective and the criminal – like Sherlock Holmes and Professor Moriarty. In a horror novel like *Frankenstein* they are Victor Frankenstein and the monster. In a romance like *Pride and Prejudice* they are the lovers, Elizabeth Bennett and Darcy.

Bond's battle with the squid (a plot point also called "the visit to death") dramatizes the fullest conflict of the adversarial forces: all of Bond's resources of strength and cunning are pitted against the most monstrous embodiment of Dr. No's sadism. This scene is, of course, fictional light-years away from Jane Austen, but is structurally analogous to Elizabeth Bennett's crisis when Lydia runs off with Wickham. For the crisis precedes the resolution of the drama and makes it possible. In *Pride and Prejudice* Darcy facilitates Lydia's marriage to Wickham and so precipitates his own marriage to Elizabeth. Just so, as we'll see a little later, Ian Fleming designed his plot so that Bond's battle with the squid –

the summit of Freytag's dramatic pyramid – would bring about the conclusion of his story.

But for now let's go back to see how – after he triggered the conflict of adversaries in the opening three chapters – Ian Fleming plotted the rising action of Bond's adventures in Jamaica. What we find out – in a nutshell – is that Fleming carefully planned to escalate this conflict and build suspense by constructing the next three chapters around several increasingly menacing danger signals that are followed by outright attacks. He does this, in large measure, through the introduction of secondary characters who function as surrogates for Bond and Dr. No. It is as if, in a game of chess, it is the pawns – and not the kings – who fight the preliminary battles.

As soon as Bond gets off the plane in Jamaica, the first and most important of these secondary characters makes his entrance: it is Bond's old buddy, factotum and personal trainer Quarrel. It is worth noting that Fleming, in designing the structure of his story, did not give Quarrel a merely "walk-on" part. Instead he gave Quarrel his own subplot – a story-within-the-story that advances the main action and that (as we will see) Fleming placed strategically for the greatest dramatic impact. In doing so he modified and recycled one of his earlier experiments in plotting. For Quarrel's subplot is an adaptation of the same plotting mechanism Fleming had used in *From Russia with Love* – the story of James Bond's friend and fellow secret agent, the amiable and doomed Darko Kerim.

Within a page of meeting the likeable Quarrel at the airport we also meet his evil counterpart -- the " pretty Chinese girl in Jamaican dress" who tries to takes Bond's picture and tricks him into telling her the name of his hotel. Although Bond immediately suspects the girl's motive, he is -- at this point -- only "vaguely worried." But then -- as soon as Bond and Quarrel leave the airport -- a mysterious black taxi follows them. With these very small details of his plot, Fleming has promised us future conflict. He doesn't wait very long – only a few pages – before he makes good on that promise by giving us overt violence. For the beautiful Chinese girl with the camera soon reappears in a local restaurant and -- refusing to name her employer – slashes Quarrel's face with a broken flashbulb. "He'll get you, you bastards!" she says. And now the notes of menace grow louder and more frequent.

One of Quarrel's most important structural functions in the novel is to serve as a conduit for these danger signals: it is from Quarrel that Bond learns that Dr. No's island is "a bad luck place" and that Dr. No will kill anyone who interferes with him. Bond sees Quarrel's palpable fear as itself a significant barometer of danger. It is Quarrel, moreover, who introduces Bond to the restaurant-owner who had been maimed by a giant octopus in the waters off Crab Key – an apparently minor plot detail that Fleming carefully placed early in the story as a foreshadowing of Bond's later encounter with the giant squid.

Fleming placed another important danger signal as the climax – the zinger – of Chapter Five. Bond – who by now has realized that Strangways and his assistant have not run off on a romantic holiday tryst but been murdered – has gone to the Colonial Office to ask about Dr. No. The person from whom Bond learns the most is the colonial secretary, a likeable fellow named Pleydell-Smith, the kind of fictional puppet that Henry James calls a "ficelle" – a minor character whose basic purpose is to provide necessary information dramatically. A faint alarm sounds just after Pleydell-Smith shakes Bond's hand and offers him a chair: Pleydell-Smith has read Bond's file because he'd found it "lying around the other day." At first troubled to hear that his file had just been "lying around" – concerned that someone might be snooping on him – Bond feels reassurred when Pleydell-Smith remembers that he'd found the file lying among "plenty of other files" on his secretary's desk. Rendered in a few paragraphs of pleasant, easy dialogue between Bond and Pleydell-Smith, this is the set-up for Bond's grim smile of recognition – the turning point –that Fleming reserved for the very end of the chapter. For now Bond sees that Pleydell-Smith's secretary is, like the young woman who slashed Quarrel's face with a flashbulb, a pretty Chinese girl who is Dr. No's pawn.

    Fleming obviously planned to have these merely menacing events of chapters four and five build up to the murderous attacks of chapter six. The first of these is the poisoned fruit that Bond finds waiting for him in his hotel room. The second is the deadly centipede that Bond discovers crawling on him as he lies in bed -- a delightfully horrible scene that Fleming reserved both as the climax of this three-chapter sequence and as the suspenseful prelude to Bond's and Quarrel's night voyage to Crab Island.

News of a third attempt on his life reaches Bond in Chapter Seven, just as they are about to set sail: two look-alikes he has hired to impersonate him and Quarrel have been violently killed. Up to this point in the plot, Bond has been reactive – observing the danger signals, gathering information like a detective. But now that the attacks by the unseen enemy have reached a climax of malice and monstrosity, Bond changes from reactive to pro-active. As he prepares to confront the enemy on Crab Key, the perceptive detective transforms into the action hero.

When Quarrel agrees to go with Bond to Crab Key, he asks Bond to buy him life insurance. This is just one example of how Fleming has mined his plot with the fictional equivalent of time-bombs that he sets to explode at the most dramatic moment. Another example is the hiring of the look-alikes in Chapter Five so that they can die to the greatest effect in Chapter Seven.
Still another is the story that M tells in Chapter Three about the man burned to death by a fire-breathing dragon -- a way that Fleming baits the novel's opening hook with a mystery that turns out to be a fundamental element of the Quarrel subplot. Quarrel's asking Bond for life insurance is, of course, a tip-off that Fleming has designed him not just as a barometer of danger but as a likeable time-bomb.

By the end of Chapter Six, Fleming has structured his novel like two acts of a drama – two three-chapter sequences, each of which has built to an important turning point: at the end of the first sequence Bond accepted his assignment; at the end of the second sequence, Dr. No's outright attacks have propelled Bond into action. Chapter Seven (the "Night Passage" to Crab Key) – a journey to the land of death and danger -- seems to have been designed as a narrative bridge before the curtain rises on act three.

Fleming opens this act by introducing one of his typical Bond-meets-gorgeous-girl subplots: as Bond wakes up on a beach, he sees the beautiful and naked Honeychile Rider gathering seashells by the water's edge. Up until now Fleming has built suspense into his plot in two fundamental ways – by creating a mystery and by tantalizing his reader with foretastes of future violence. Now he has raised the stakes with the promise of sex. Just as soon as Fleming has done this – shown us Bond's flirtation with the naked girl – he ties their romance to the main plot of mystery and danger.

The important point here is that the romantic subplot is not a divergence from the main plot, but instead advances it. Bond and Quarrel have managed to land on Crab Key unnoticed, because their canoe has evaded Dr. No's radar. But Honey also has a canoe – and now Dr. No's henchmen have spotted it and mistaken it for Bond's. So her arrival on the island unintentionally triggers an attack by Bond's dangerous adversary. By tying the Honey-Bond romance to the main plot in this way, Fleming found a way to plan a chapter that opens with erotic titillation but ends with a cliff-hanger that promises danger ahead. "Quick cap'n," says Quarrel: "Dey's a comin'."

Fleming clearly planned his next chapters on Crab Key so that two of his drivers of suspense -- titillation and impending danger – would work together to make readers turn the page. When Dr. No's flunkies strafe the beach with machine-gun fire, Bond and the naked girl must snuggle closer together in their foxhole. As their enemy closes in on them and they must wade together up a river, Bond has no choice but to take off his pants: "Honey, we can't be shy on this trip," he says. And yet Fleming is careful to increase – and not release – this provocative sexual suspense. When Honey invites Bond into her sleeping bag, Bond (who has scruples about violating her innocence) gently declines her offer. Not taking no for an answer, Honey makes Bond promise that they will sleep together when they get back to Jamaica: "Now you owe me slave-time," she says.

By the time Bond is savoring Honey's "warm animal smell" as they share their romantic interlude beside the lake on Crab Key, the reader has reached the middle of the book – and still not met Dr. No. This fact says a lot about Fleming's main strategy for building up mystery and suspense. Up until now all of the evil characters – the three blindmen who killed Strangways and Mary Trueblood, the Chinese girls on Jamaica, the unseen "messenger" who left poison and a deadly centipede in Bond's hotel room, the men on the boat firing their machine guns at the beach – have been Dr. No's surrogates. Since this is so, it seems reasonable to conclude that one of Fleming's very first decisions when he worked out the plot for this novel was to keep Dr. No offstage for as long as possible: by so doing he could ratchet up the mystery. Two other decisions must have followed as logical consequences of this first decision to hide Dr. No from the reader until the last third of the book: it would be necessary to create a number of minor villains who would be Dr. No's stand-ins until the criminal mastermind himself walks onstage; and it would be necessary to make Dr. No's entrance sufficiently dramatic.

    It is obviously for the latter purpose that Fleming planned to have Quarrel get burned to death by the mechanical "fire breathing dragon" – the grisly act-three climax that immediately precedes Bond's and Honey's capture by Dr. No's henchmen. Evidently it was in order to create this major plot point as a dramatic prelude to Dr. No's appearance in the story that Fleming decided to give Quarrel so much time onstage. This is also why Fleming introduced the "dragon" mystery in his first act and later had Honey reintroduce it just a few chapters before the so-called "dragon" incinerates Quarrel. What we as writers should bear in mind here is the evident care with which Fleming planned this climax in advance – separately spinning out two of his plot strands (the Quarrel subplot and the "dragon" mystery) until he makes them violently converge. Fleming designed the five-chapter sequence that is the third act of his drama so that it would build to this gruesome and dangerous turn of events – so far the most dangerous moment in his story.

As the curtain rises on act four, Bond and Honey have just arrived at Dr. No's mountain fortress. Surprised by the luxurious accommodations and a charade of welcome (instead of the horrors they expected), they are soon escorted to their bedroom. In the midst of some soft pornographic passages that keep the prurient reader turning pages, Bond eats breakfast – and soon realizes that he's been drugged. It is only now that Dr. No finally appears onstage for the very first time – as he creeps into their bedroom and examines his captives while they're sleeping. The casual reader, curious to join Bond and Honey as they dine with Dr. No in the next chapter, won't pause to ask why Fleming chose to situate Dr. No's entrance at this position in his plot. But we plot-builders must ask.

The answer becomes apparent when we take a look at the quick succession of events that now unfold. Immediately after Dr. No's first appearance, Bond and Honey meet with him for dinner – after which Dr. No sentences them to their respective tortures: the naked Honey is to be "pegged out" and eaten alive by crabs; Bond will be forced to endure a progression of agonies that culminate in his encounter with the giant squid. Dr. No's first entrance, in other words, leads directly and quickly to the obligatory scene. It seems likely, then, that Fleming must have reached the conclusion that the very best moment for Dr. No's first appearance would have to be just a few chapters before the novel's obligatory scene – the decisive battle between the good and evil forces.

For by placing these two major plot points in such close succession he could maximize their dramatic pressure.

A good way to visualize this placement of Dr. No's first entrance would be to think of Freytag's pyramid. If the top of Freytag's pyramid is the obligatory scene (the crisis), then Bond's battle with the squid is the summit of the pyramid and Dr. No's entrance is located just below it on the rising incline. From the vantage point afforded by this elevation on the pyramid, we can now look back down at the rising conflict that preceded it. What we can see from up here is that Fleming designed his plot so that the escalation of the conflict would bring the antagonists geographically closer and closer together. Down at the bottom of the pyramid (the presentation of the so-called "story problem," when Bond is in London accepting his assignment) the antagonists are as far apart as possible -- and Bond is not at all in danger. When Bond goes to Jamaica and begins his investigation (as he climbs higher and higher up the pyramid) the antagonists are closer together -- and Bond is increasingly threatened. When Bond arrives on Crab Key (climbing still higher up the pyramid) the adversaries are geographically even closer – and Bond is in greater danger than ever before. It is not until just before the moment of Bond's maximum danger – the obligatory scene -- that the antagonists meet face to face. This plan to increase danger (and therefore suspense) while simultaneously bringing his antagonists geographically closer and closer to one another must have been one of Fleming's fundamental strategies when plotting *Dr. No*.

Fleming didn't only plan Dr. No's entrance as a set-up for the obligatory scene, but also as a prelude to the crisis of the romantic subplot. For that – structurally speaking – is what Honey's exposure to the crabs is: her decisive life-or-death moment and the great trial for the "lovers." "Will it hurt?" asks Honey just before she is subjected to her ordeal. "Of course it will hurt," responds Dr. No: "I am interested in pain." As this snippet of dialogue makes obvious, Bond's and Honey's romantic crisis can't be taken too seriously -- any more than we can feel too seriously concerned about the villainy of Dr. No. This is worth pointing out because the tongue-in-cheek, fairytale peculiarity of Fleming's fictional world has a lot to do with the kind of events he chose – and did not choose -- as key moments in his plot.

Dr. No's relatively brief appearance in the novel (wedged between Quarrel's death and Bond's "assault course against death") introduces the reader to one of Fleming's signature villains -- the personification of a bizarre evil that borders on the comic. His grotesque physical attributes (like his steel claws, his glass eyes and his heart on the wrong side of his body) and his equally ludicrous pursuits (like hijacking guided missiles while amassing millions from the sale of bird dung) combine to create a caricature whose evil is an under-stated joke. The villainous fun of his dinner conversation with Bond doesn't only set up the twin crises of the main plot and of the romantic subplot, but also unravels the novel's central mystery: the reason why Strangways and Mary Trueblood were murdered in the opening chapter.

The details of the plot here (that Strangways had been killed because he suspected Dr. No's evil machinations) are less important than the fact that Fleming has married the escalating suspense of a thriller to the story-building conventions of a murder mystery – presenting a murder at the beginning of his drama and revealing the motives for the murder toward the end. But the fact that the motives for the murder – and the villain himself – are not revealed until late in the novel shouldn't mislead us plot-builders about the order in which these central story-elements were created. For although the reader typically discovers the villain and his motives in the final chapters of a crime story, the writer (in this case Ian Fleming) does just the opposite: getting to know the villain (or antagonist) is the very first step in the process of dreaming up a plot. This is so because the antagonist in any drama is truly the plot-maker, the author's surrogate within the fiction. Dr. No's murder of Strangways, for example, is the incident (the triggering event) that sets the entire machinery of the novel into motion: Dr. No, in other words, is not just the villain -- but also the prime mover of the story.

Fleming planned Dr. No's long-awaited appearance onstage as Bond's moment of supreme danger. But the nature of the danger that awaits Bond is presented -- both to Bond and to the reader – as a mystery. "It is," says Dr. No, "the unknown dangers that are the worst." The obstacle course of horrors that Bond endures while crawling through a tunnel in Dr. No's mountain fortress is a paradigm of Fleming's technique of merging mystery with suspense. For here – as throughout the novel –

Fleming pursues a two-fold strategy of repeatedly threatening Bond while at the same time making sure that danger is always inseparable from the unknown. As he begins to crawl through the tunnel, Bond does not know that burning metal walls and tarantulas await him – or what greater terror he will face in the "killing ground." The curious reader turns the page, drawn on by the promise of danger and the mystery of the unknown.

Because the dangers that lie ahead of Bond in the tunnel are unknown, the reader is surprised each time Bond comes upon a new one. Each surprise is followed by renewed curiosity. After Bond survives the climb up the vertical shaft, and after he stabs the tarantulas with his knife, the reader wonders: what will happen next? By specifically describing a succession of unexpected ordeals that Bond endures in the tunnel and his growing dread of a final ordeal ahead, Fleming carefully builds the reader's curiosity in order to gratify it with the even greater surprise of the obligatory scene – Bond's battle with the giant squid. This scene is "obligatory" because the novel's opening sequence (Dr. No's opening gambit answered by Bond's embarking on his quest) has led the reader to expect just such a showdown between the antagonists. Like Odysseus blinding the Cyclops, Bond plunges his spear into the monster's eyeball – the major turning point of the plot that we might also call the "Act Four Crisis," the apex of the Freytag's pyramid or (if you're one of Aristotle's groupies) the *peripateia*.

This major reversal now precipitates the next major plot point – the climax. Bond (whom Dr. No has never expected to survive) now has the advantage of surprise.

So he is able to creep unseen down to the shipyard, commandeer a crane . . . and dump its load of bird manure on his enemy. Dr. No's semi-comic demise comes just a few pages after Bond's battle with the squid: the novel's crisis and climax strike in close succession like a one-two punch. And then -- after only one page of suspense fueled by the new danger that one of Dr. No's goons might notice Bond's escape – the resolution of the romantic subplot unexpectedly begins.

    While each is trying to escape, Bond and Honey mistake one another for enemies, fight -- recognize one another and are reunited. The half dozen short paragraphs in which Fleming renders this turning-point are themselves worth pausing over because they exemplify his dramatic method. First Fleming (as he characteristically does) creates tension by threatening Bond with an unknown danger – in this case Dr. No's henchman whom Bond fears might come upon him and attack him as he tries to escape. Then Fleming subjects Bond to just such an attack -- an event that heightens the narrative tension at the same time as it surprises the reader. Fleming concludes this dramatic sequence – and delivers the revelation – when Bond's attacker turns out to be Honey: she has mistaken him for an enemy, just as he has mistaken her. The casual reader will only be entertained and taken along by this progressive sequence of suspense and surprise. But we writers should study the method.

    The rapid sequence of plot points – crisis, climax, reunion of the lovers -- is the movement down the other side of Freytag's pyramid, the quickly falling action of the drama. While dangerous conflict had been rising all the way up the plot pyramid, now the process is reversed. In keeping with this pattern of reversal, the fire-breathing "dragon" that killed Quarrel now turns out to be the vehicle that carries Bond and Honey to safety. The step-by-step escalation of suspense – that fuels the majority of the novel -- has suddenly given way to the mood of comedy. Just as Dr. No's burial in bird dung is understatedly comic, so is the resolution of Honey's life-or-death crisis: it turns out that the crabs haven't eaten her because they are vegetarians.

A less accomplished writer than Ian Fleming might possibly have ended the book at the moment when Bond and Honey escape from Dr. No's myrmidons and kiss. But Fleming knew better: not only that the story required an official wrap-up of the Strangways case, but – much more importantly – a delicate consummation of Bond and Honey's love story. For, in writing *Dr. No*, Fleming was forging a composite genre – combining the suspense of a thriller and the mystery of crime fiction with the kind of romantic bliss that concludes a Shakespearean comedy or an Austen novel. And so, in the final chapter of the novel, Bond attends an official meeting in Jamaica, sends a telegram to M and – in a disarmingly touching scene – makes love to Honey.

So Bond has accomplished his mission – solved the mystery of Strangways' disappearance and killed an evil genius whose ability to re-direct guided missiles might have destroyed mankind. In the process he has survived poison, a deadly centipede, a giant squid and a number of murderous goons he has either knifed or shot. He has been tortured with burning metal and tarantulas, been a helpless eyewitness to the murder of an old friend and made passionate love to a breath-taking beauty. But – after all this -- has Bond changed: has he grown inwardly as a character? Of course not. Then how is it that *Dr. No* is such a good story?

By constructing his plot around warring opposites, Fleming has created a fictional world where conflict is completely external. All of the major moments of change – the plot points – are changes in the dynamics of this external conflict. We can see that this is so when we recall the most important dramatic moments of the story: Bond's accepting his assignment, the increasingly loud danger alarms of the Jamaica chapters, Quarrel's murder, Bond's dinner with Dr. No, his ordeal in the tunnel, his battle with the squid and – finally – his victory over his enemy. Each of these plot events is a moment in the external conflict between Bond and Dr. No. As this external conflict builds, it confronts Bond with greater and greater external danger. Mounting danger and mystery-story conventions (like an unsolved murder and an elusive villain) generate suspense and curiosity that together make readers turn the page. But not one of these plot points is a moment in a drama of internal conflict for Bond or for any of the other characters. Nor is any one of the many moments of surprise with which Fleming has mined his plot an instance of sudden internal understanding – the kind of coming-to-realize moment we see, for example, at the end of Joyce's *Araby*. Instead revelation is the sudden understanding that occurs when the unknown danger turns out to be an octopus. James Bond doesn't have epiphanies.

That is because Bond is blissfully free of internal conflict. He is marvelously unperplexed. This is not to say that Fleming has not – to some extent – given Bond an internal life. For example, Fleming allows Bond (in the last chapter of the novel) a few moments of nostalgic reverie about Quarrel. Bond can feel protective toward a woman, can admire a beautiful sunset or feel resentful toward M for giving him a supposedly "cushy assignment." These are the kinds of details that give life to fiction. But they are not plot points: they are not moments of dramatic change.

A lot is said in the plot books about the need to create a backstory for one's characters. But James Bond is successfully propelled through adventure after adventure without almost any backstory at all. Instead Fleming endowed Bond with (so to speak) a selective amnesia. In *Dr. No* Bond can remember M and the sound of gunfire in the Ardennes -- and pauses for a moment on a beach to wonder what became of Solitaire (his love interest in *Live and Let Die*). But he does not give even a moment's thought to Tatiana Romanova -- his "darling" in *From Russia with Love*. That is not because Bond is a cad. No, Bond is always chivalrous. It's just that his memory is oddly incomplete. If Bond feels any regret at the beginning of *Dr. No*, it is not for the loss of his last love, Tatiana Romanova – but for the loss of his Beretta.

Dr. No is a page-turner: the reason why readers don't give a hoot whether Bond and the other characters grow or not is that Fleming (from the first chapter on) has defined conflict as entirely external. The reason why this is so instructive for those of us who set out to make plots of our own is that the example of *Dr. No* illustrates the importance of asking ourselves – at the outset of our work – where we will locate conflict. Will the heart be the battleground? Or will (as in *Dr. No*) the battle be external? Or will the war be waged on both fronts? For a plot is a system of dynamic change, a page-turning machine whose onward movement is fueled by conflict. The key events are the major turning points in this conflict – and the crafting of these events (the choice of which incidents are crucial) will depend on the kind and the location of the conflict. Conflicts of the heart require changes of heart. Conflicts between indestructible secret agents and semi-comic super-villains do not. James Bond doesn't change because he doesn't have to.

    A major advantage of Fleming's strategy of pitting Bond against a megalomaniacal super-villain is that danger – the rocket fuel of suspense – is always an abundant resource. But, inevitably, there is something unreal about such a purely external conflict. That is why Fleming's characters (who play their parts very well without being overburdened by the problems of an inner life) are exaggerations like the caricatures in a comic book. Honeychile Rider and Tatiana Romanova and Pussy Galore are as two-dimensional as are Bond's ludicrous enemies – like Oddjob with his murderous bowler hat, like Rosa Klebb with her knife-toed boots, like Red Grant who must kill when the moon is full. We are not supposed to take them too seriously. A Bond adventure isn't a novel of manners like *Pride and*

Prejudice. It is an elegant entertainment like a martini – shaken, not stirred.

Pride, Prejudice and Plot-Making

"While the laws of living movement go forward from cause to effect, the laws of volitional representation go *backward*, from effect to cause."
    -- John Howard Lawson, *Theory and Technique of Playwriting*

   Since writing backwards, planning a story from effects to causes, is one of the most important weapons in the plot-maker's arsenal, let's start out by taking a look at how *Pride and Prejudice* ends. The novel, of course, concludes with Elizabeth Bennet's marriage to Darcy. It is probably the most famous example of the kind of plot finale that John Truby calls the "double reversal" – an ending where the protagonist and antagonist bring about each other's transformation. Unlike a Bond novel, where conflict is located externally, the conflict in *Pride and Prejudice* is situated internally and the major function of the plot is first to create that conflict and then to resolve it in the mutual transformation of the lovers – in the overcoming of Darcy's pride and Elizabeth Bennet's prejudice. Three major events precipitate their romantic metamorphosis: Lydia and Wickham's marriage, Jane and Bingley's marriage and, ironically, Lady Catherine de Bourg's scandalized and unsuccessful attempt to persuade Darcy not to marry Elizabeth.
   Each of these three events is the culmination of a separate subplot that, since the opening chapters of the novel, has been interwoven with the others, repeatedly crisscrossing, interrupting and bringing conflict to the

main story thread about the judgments and feelings of Elizabeth and Darcy. Together with the part played by the Gardiners (Elizabeth's worthy aunt and uncle who bring her to Pemberley at the beginning of Volume III), these three major events and the Elizabeth-Darcy marriage that follows them together comprise that part of the plot that the French call the *denouement*, a word that in English literally means "untying" – or, better yet, "unknotting."

    Anyone who has read the book (or seen the movie) will remember this untying of knot after knot. Jane's letter to Elizabeth relating the disastrous news that Lydia has eloped with Wickham arrives just when things are finally beginning to go well for Elizabeth and Darcy. Austen, in other words, has chosen to place the novel's major reversal – the crisis – at a high point for the main plot. It comes when Elizabeth has begun to see that she is mistaken about Darcy's pride – after Darcy has invited her uncle to go fishing and has introduced her to his sister Georgiana. Even Bingley's reappearance to greet Elizabeth at the inn suggests that Jane's romantic prospects are at last looking better. But now the news of Lydia's disgrace changes everything for both Elizabeth and Jane. The dramatic effect is the literary equivalent of a sudden rush downhill in a roller coaster.

    As a plotting convention the crisis (a.k.a. the "obligatory scene") is the dark moment of decisive battle between the warring opposites of the drama.
In an externally located conflict like an Ian Fleming novel the warring opposites are James Bond and a super-villain – and the crisis is, for example a battle with a

squid. But in an internally located conflict like an Austen novel the warring opposites are within the protagonists themselves – and the crisis (like Lydia's elopement with Wickham) is a dilemma that forces them to do battle with their own demons. In their own different ways Lydia and Wickham personify those demons: Lydia as a silly, thoughtless embodiment of the Bennet family's shame; and Wickham both as a source of mortification for Elizabeth and as a Darcy family nemesis. Up until the moment when Elizabeth reads Jane's letter telling of their elopement, Lydia and Wickham have each been woven – separately – into the narrative. But now their joining together comes as an explosive and unpleasant surprise.

The major reason why the crisis of *Pride and Prejudice* is so instructive for novelists is that it tells us something crucial about the order of the steps that Austen took as she worked out the structure of her plot. It tells us, in a nutshell, that she planned her crisis first and then worked backward. This becomes obvious when we realize that it is only by looking backward from the vantage point of the crisis that it is possible to see how its complex effect upon both Elizabeth and Darcy depends upon the carefully planned plot events that have preceded it.

Elizabeth has two basically different and simultaneous reactions to the news that Lydia has run off with Wickham -- she feels mortified and is also certain for the first time that she loves Darcy: "never had she so honestly felt that she could have loved him, as now, when all love must be vain." The reason, of course, why she feels that "all love must be vain" is because she believes that now Darcy's pride will stand in between them. Part of her mortification comes from the fact that – for two reasons -- she can no longer fault him for his pride. First of all, Lydia's disgrace forces Elizabeth to recognize the justice of Darcy's objection to her family's "total want of propriety." But a second – and perhaps even more painful reason – is that Lydia has disgraced herself with Wickham: "Brother-in-law of Wickham! Every kind of pride must revolt from the connection."

   Elizabeth's mortification when Lydia runs off with Wickham depends for much of its impact upon her previous infatuation with Wickham and consequent disparagement of Darcy in Volume 1 and the first half of Volume II. Austen, in other words, had to set up Elizabeth's shame by inventing preceding incidents that would fuel the power of her heroine's pained understanding at the crisis. Austen also had to set up Elizabeth's mortification at the crisis by inventing the earlier episodes that involve Lydia's running after officers -- as well as all of the other incidents (like those with Mrs. Bennet) that demonstrate the Bennet family's foolishness. Darcy's urging Bingley to break off his romance with Jane is yet another incident that Austen had to invent as an early complication of the plot in order to increase Elizabeth's distress at the crisis. After all, if the Bennet family fiasco at the Netherfield ball was enough of a reason for Darcy to urge Bingley not to marry Jane, then Lydia's running off with Wickham brings even greater disgrace to the Bennet family and is therefore a doubly persuasive reason why Elizabeth feels certain that Darcy will no longer want to marry her.

The role that Wickham plays at the crisis affects Elizabeth and Darcy differently. For Elizabeth the deceptively attractive Wickham is a source of shame that makes her see how wrong – how prejudiced – she has been. But for Darcy the hated Wickham is the cause of the decisive battle between pride and love. The outcome of this battle – Darcy's choice of love over pride – can only be understood in the context of plot events that have preceded the crisis. In other words, just as Austen had to plot backwards for Elizabeth, so she had to plot backwards for Darcy. She must first have decided how each would react to the crisis – and only then have invented the earlier incidents that would make their reactions meaningful. In order, for example, to establish the meaning of what Darcy does for Elizabeth – his negotiating and paying for Lydia's marriage to Wickham – it was necessary for Austen to plot all the earlier events that establish Darcy's pride and explain his hatred for Wickham.

After first deciding that the crisis would be the major battle in Darcy's internal conflict (the dilemma that would force him to decide whether his love for Elizabeth is stronger than his pride), Austen's second step would have been to figure out just exactly what Wickham had done to Darcy – what kind of transgression would have been the greatest affront to Darcy's pride. So, plotting backward from the crisis, Austen must have then invented the backstory about Wickham's attempted seduction of Darcy's sister Georgiana. Austen's invention of this detail of her plot is, of course, one more example of how novelists are always modifying and recycling characters and dramatic situations they have used before. For the idea that Wickham had tried to corrupt Darcy's sister is evidently a reworking of a similar story thread in *Sense and Sensibility*: the handsome but unworthy Willoughby's seduction and abandonment of Colonel Brandon's fifteen-year-old ward.

Austen's decision to cast Wickham as the villain of the crisis-- as a source of mortification for Elizabeth and as the chief antagonist in Darcy's battle against his pride -- must have been among the very first she made when designing the structure of her plot. All of the plot events in volumes one and two that involve Wickham (Lydia's flirtation with officers, Elizabeth's infatuation with Wickham and Darcy's mysterious hatred of him) could only have been improvised as a consequence of this decision and not before. The storyline that centers upon Wickham (and comes to include Lydia) is one of the three subplots of the novel that at first complicate and later combine to bring about the resolution of the main plot of the novel – the story of Elizabeth Bennet and Darcy. When Darcy chooses love over pride by arranging Lydia and Wickham's marriage, he concludes the crisis – the first of the three major plot events that initiate the novel's denouement. Almost immediately (after the married Wickham and Lydia have visited the Bennet family) the unknotting of a second subplot – the Jane-Bingley romance – begins.

After his long absence from Netherfield, Bingley returns to visit Jane – and brings Darcy along with him. At once Elizabeth begins to hope that Darcy's "affection and wishes must still be unshaken." Jane and Bingley's happy ending, in other words, ushers in a happy ending for Elizabeth and Darcy. What we plot-builders shouldn't miss here – and any place throughout the novel where the stories of the two sisters' romances are intertwined – is that the fortunes of the two couples are mutually dependent. Each either impedes or advances the other. Darcy (because he had witnessed the Bennet family's disgraceful behavior at the Netherfield Ball and had mistakenly believed that Jane was indifferent to Bingley) had advised his friend to break off with Elizabeth's sister. So up until the happy ending Darcy has been what has often been called a "blocking figure" who gets in the way of Jane's romance with Bingley. But the Jane-and-Bingley subplot has also – until the novel's denouement – blocked the Elizabeth-and-Darcy romance. After all, Darcy's interference in Jane's romance is the major reason why Elizabeth angrily turns down his first proposal -- a major turning point that (as we'll see more fully later on) takes place at the very middle of the novel.

    When Austen first started plotting *Pride and Prejudice*, she undoubtedly knew that her story would end with the marriage of both sisters. For that's just exactly how she'd ended *Sense and Sensibility*, a book that in many respects reads like a first draft of the other. Starting out with the knowledge that the two oldest Bennet sisters (like the two oldest Dashwood sisters) would both be married at the end, she then had to plot backward from this "unknotting" and tie as many knots as possible.

The first of the knots she had to tie was at the ball (Volume 1, Chapter III) where Elizabeth and Jane meet Darcy and Bingley -- a scene that is the reversed mirror image of the sisters' happy ending. For the dance where Darcy's pride sparks Elizabeth's prejudice and where Jane and Bingley begin to fall in love not only initiates and interconnects the main plot and the subplot, but also sets the stage for both couples' romantic problems. The love between the sisters and the friendship between the men – particularly Bingley's reliance on Darcy's judgment – is the bond that makes these two romantic storylines rise and fall in tandem. The second dance in Volume 1, the Netherfield Ball, is where Austen tied both couples into a double knot.
For Darcy's interference in Jane and Bingley's romance is the major complication in Volume One.

But in Volume III these knots are untied: Darcy apologizes for his interference and Bingley proposes to Jane. In the very next chapter Lady Catherine de Bourgh arrives -- unexpectedly and uninvited -- at the Bennet house. This confrontation between Lady Catherine's ludicrously haughty outrage and Elizabeth Bennet's self-possessed strength is the third of the three major plot events that combine to bring about Elizabeth and Darcy's romantic transformation. It is only from the vantage point afforded by this chapter -- by looking backward over the story events that have preceded it -- that it is possible to see that this dramatic encounter is one more piece of evidence that Austen plotted in reverse. She must have planned this scene first -- and only then have plotted the earlier events that would lead up to it. By working in reverse from effects to causes, she plotted a sequence of preceding incidents so that Elizabeth's showdown with Lady Catherine would become the explosive finale of the subplot set in motion by the ridiculous Mr. Collins.

After all, when we as readers first meet Collins we don't know where his story thread is leading us. At first (although we do also incidentally learn that his patroness is Lady Catherine de Bourgh) Collins is presented to the reader mainly as the heir to the Bennet family's property and as a buffoon whose marriage proposal to Elizabeth is ludicrously unacceptable. When Collins first walks onstage, in other words, his major function in the novel's structure is carefully hidden from view. But then, after Elizabeth turns down Collins' proposal and her friend Charlotte marries him instead, the Collins subplot begins to head toward its final destination. For it is now that Charlotte invites Elizabeth to visit her at her new home in the Parsonage -- -- which adjoins the estate of Lady Catherine de Bourgh. By the time that Elizabeth is staying as a house guest at the Parsonage (visiting Lady Catherine at Rosings, where once again she encounters Darcy) it is clear that Austen has designed this subplot to advance the main plot and that Collins' principal purpose in the novel has been to serve as Lady Catherine's sycophantic harbinger.

Lady Catherine is clearly another example of a blocking figure. Her role as the major blocking figure to the main plot depends upon her ability (as Elizabeth says of her) to address Darcy "on his weakest side."

Austen planned the Collins subplot so that it would lead straight to her while setting her up as an epitome of pride -- a caricature of the pride that Darcy has been battling within himself. Lady Catherine's confrontation with Elizabeth is the crisis of this subplot – Lady Catherine's moment of decisive battle. It is (like Lydia's elopement with Wickham) another test of whether Darcy's pride or his love will predominate. As a plotting tactic, one purpose of this test is to create suspense by putting Elizabeth in a state of pained uncertainty. For this is Elizabeth's state of mind just after Lady Catherine drives away in her carriage – "some uneasiness" that Lady Catherine's arguments might appeal to Darcy's "notions of dignity" and so prevent their marriage. Her fear that Lady Catherine might persuade Darcy to abandon her is Elizabeth's final misperception of him, the lingering shadow of her prejudice. Elizabeth remains in this agony of suspense until she sees Darcy again.

    Those of us who make up stories might benefit by pausing to consider the dramatic purpose served by this moment of pain and uncertainty just before the lovers finally come to understand one another in the last pages of the novel. It is not only a moment of pain and uncertainty for Elizabeth, but for Darcy as well. After all, the motivation that drives Darcy's participation in the other two major events of the denouement – in arranging Lydia's marriage to Wickham and in furthering Jane's romance with Bingley -- is certainly his love for Elizabeth, but a love whose urgent activity springs from the pain and doubt caused by her refusal of his offer of marriage. Romantic pain in a love story (the structural equivalent of danger in a thriller) doesn't only fuel the suspense that makes readers turn the page: it also sweetens the happy ending.

While Austen apparently plotted backwards so that the incidents involving Collins would be a set-up for the confrontation scene between Lady Catherine and Elizabeth, she designed the confrontation scene itself as a set-up for the final ironic reversal that would bring Elizabeth and Darcy to their "present good understanding." Austen engineered this ironic reversal by making Darcy's reaction to Lady Catherine's "conversation" with Elizabeth just the opposite of what Elizabeth has feared and of what his aunt has intended. "It taught me to hope," says Darcy, "as I had scarcely ever allowed myself to hope before."

With these words Lady Catherine has lost her battle. If one were to graph the fortunes of the characters, then Elizabeth and Darcy's trajectory has just soared upward, while Lady Catherine's has taken a nosedive. Story-makers can learn a lot from this technique of creating irony by making interweaving plotlines move in opposite directions – the same kind of ironic counterpoint between story threads that Austen wove into the crisis, where Lydia's silly glee is the source of Elizabeth's torment.

As a blocking figure whose purpose in the structure of the story is to keep Elizabeth and Darcy apart, Lady Catherine is not so much an external obstacle as an internal impediment -- a ludicrous figure of pride who obstructs their ability to see one another clearly. Her defeat is an ironic exorcism that adds surprise and comedy to the final vision of romantic bliss.

Following in close succession after Lydia and Wickham's marriage and then after Bingley's proposal to Jane, Lady Catherine's ironic overthrow is the third of the major story events that combine to usher in the happy resolution of the main plot. Each of these three major events is the unknotting of a subplot, a turning point from which Austen apparently plotted backward in order to invent a sequence of incidents that would lead up to it. The three subplots become unknotted, one after another, and together unknot the main plot. The power of this unknotting in the denouement derives from the tightness of the knots that have preceded it.

The tightest of the knots – the lowest point for the main plot – occurs at the very middle of the novel when Elizabeth angrily turns down Darcy's first proposal. This dramatic nadir comes directly after Elizabeth learns from Colonel Fitzwilliam that Darcy persuaded Bingley to break off his romance with Jane. Austen carefully planted this revelation at the moment in her story when it could do the most damage to the Elizabeth-and-Darcy romance: for Elizabeth now knows that Darcy is the sole cause of her sister's unhappiness. Colonel Fitzwilliam exists as a character only for the purpose of making this unintentional disclosure – that infuriates Elizabeth's and so sets the stage for her refusing Darcy's first offer of marriage.

All three of the subplots contribute toward bringing about this central downturn in the main plot – a romantic debacle that takes place while Darcy is visiting his aunt and Elizabeth is nearby, visiting her friend Charlotte. Evidently one of the major reasons why Austen created Lady Catherine's subplot was as an expedient for bringing Elizabeth and Darcy into physical proximity. But a second reason is the pride that Lady Catherine epitomizes and that Darcy is now struggling against. Elizabeth first explains her refusal by pointing out that Darcy has said he liked her against his "will," against his "reason" and "even against" his "character." To this she adds that he has injured her sister and that Wickham has spoken against his character. All of the preceding incidents that involve Wickham – Elizabeth's attraction to him and her belief in his lies about Darcy -- have been designed to lead up to the moment when she angrily rejects Darcy's proposal. But it is Jane's subplot, the revelation that Darcy is the cause of Jane's romantic problems, that is the immediate cause of Elizabeth's refusal.

Colonel Fitzwilliam's revelation that Darcy had "saved" Bingley from an "imprudent marriage" to Jane is the third of a three-step sequence of crucial events that Austen invented in order to make the crisis in Jane's subplot impact the main plot and bring it to its lowest point. The first step in this sequence occurs during the Netherfield Ball, when Mrs. Bennet's disgraceful behavior convinces Darcy that he must separate Bingley from Jane. The second step in this sequence -- Jane's distress when Bingley unexpectedly leaves Netherfield – is the critical turning point at the end of Volume 1. Austen withholds the reason for Bingley's departure in order to fuel Colonel Fitzwilliam's explosive revelation at the midpoint of the novel.

Austen apparently first decided that Elizabeth's refusal of Darcy's proposal would be the major complication at the middle of the novel and then plotted backward to prepare the interweaving storylines that would bring it about. With this low point in view, Austen designed the initial downturn of the plot in order to increase the emotional satisfaction of the upturn that she planned for the novel's conclusion. But before plotting the downward slope of the narrative, Austen had to define her story problem – a two-part process that consists of establishing the story's goals and of introducing the forces that block the way to their achievement.

The famous opening sentence of the novel ("It is a truth universally acknowledged, that a single man in possession of a good fortune, must be in want of a wife.") immediately establishes that a financially lucrative marriage is at least part of the goal that the eldest Bennet sisters are hoping to achieve. The plainly unsatisfactory and unequal marriage of their parents – the estimable but ineffectual Mr. Bennet and his foolish wife – soon makes it clear to the reader that the sisters' goal of marriage must comprise not only money but also mutual respect. At the very same time that Austen presents this kind of worthy marriage as the sisters' goal, her portrayal of Mrs. Bennet's foolishness begins the process of introducing the forces that will impede them as they try to reach it. This process continues as Mrs. Bennet's favorite daughter – Lydia -- is introduced in the very first chapter of the novel.

Although Austen will introduce several more blocking characters as her plotlines begin to interweave, the two-fold process of presenting the novel's story problem (the presentation of a conflict between goals and impediments) is complete by the end of Chapter III, the ball where Elizabeth and Jane first meet Darcy and Bingley. For Austen establishes the goal – the marriage of each couple – at the same time that she portrays the major impediments: Darcy's pride, Elizabeth's prejudice and Bingley's reliance on his friend's "advice."

Now that Austen has plotted the opening of her fiction so that the fundamental conflict between goals and impediments is well underway, the conflict increases and the storyline begins its downward slope. The principal way that Austen builds conflict is by repeatedly demonstrating that Jane's and Elizabeth's marriage objectives are threatened by the "low" behavior of their family. This is evidently the reason why Austen invented Mrs. Bennet's garrulous foolishness and Lydia's running after officers – in order to burden Elizabeth and Jane with relatives who not only provoke and deserve contempt, but who also stand in the way of their happiness. Bingley's unpleasant sisters (who mock Mrs. Bennet and her youngest daughters) exist as minor characters for no other purpose than to drive this point home.

By the time this conflict comes to a head at the Netherfield ball, Austen has introduced Collins and Wickham, both of whom initiate a sequence of events that will present more obstacles to the goal of romantic happiness. With these subplots now underway (Collins has already set the stage for Lady Catherine's interference and Wickham has already told his damaging lies about Darcy) Austen triggers the crisis in Jane's romance with Bingley. She does this by bringing the goal of marriage into direct conflict with the impediment – in this case by having the vulgar Mrs. Bennet chatter, in Darcy's hearing, about the advantages of the match. This direct conflict provokes Darcy's decision to separate Bingley from Jane – a decision that will have disastrous consequences when, at the dark midpoint of the novel, Darcy proposes to Elizabeth. But the Netherfield ball episode (Volume 1, Chapter XVIII) is a dramatic nexus that Austen created not only in order to complicate Elizabeth's and Jane's romances, but also in order to develop the other plotlines as well. It is at the Netherfield ball that Elizabeth introduces Charlotte to Collins – an introduction that will lead to their marriage and so set in motion the string of incidents that will bring Elizabeth to their home at the Parsonage. Wickham, by his very absence, plays an important role at the Netherfield ball. His absence deepens the mystery of the enmity between him and Darcy – a mystery that Austen carefully builds in order to have Darcy's later disclosure of Wickham's villainies become a dramatic turning point, a revelation that forces Elizabeth to reevaluate her prejudice. Austen also uses this scene to set up Wickham's elopement with Lydia: for it is at the Netherfield ball that Lydia eagerly asks Mr. Denny why Wickham isn't there.

    By the end of Volume I of *Pride and Prejudice*, the main plot and the three subplots have been introduced and interwoven in order to bring the fortunes of Elizabeth and her family to a low point. Most important of all, the trajectory of the main plot – the plot that centers upon Elizabeth and Darcy – is heading downward, since Elizabeth is infatuated with Wickham and believes all the lies Wickham has told her about Darcy. Another piece of bad news is the downturn in the Jane-and-Bingley subplot: Bingley has inexplicably left Netherfield and interrupted their romance. The third subplot (the string of incidents that at first center upon Mr. Collins until they lead to Lady Catherine) is one more source of the problems – the knots -- that beset the Bennet family at the end of the first volume. Because Collins will inherit the Bennet property after Mr. Bennet's death, his marriage to Charlotte Lucas will oust Mrs. Bennet and her daughters from their home. So the Lucas family's good luck is the Bennet family's bad luck – one more example of Austen's technique of creating irony by juxtaposing interweaving plotlines that move in opposite directions. Another negative that the Collins subplot adds to the heap of troubles at the end of Volume 1 is Elizabeth's disappointment in her friend Charlotte – who, by marrying Collins, has forfeited marital happiness in exchange for financial stability.

While Austen's plotting strategy is Volume 1 is basically to present a conflict between a story goal and a variety of impediments and then to heighten this conflict so that the impediments begin to overtake the goal, her strategy in Volume II is contradictory: both to make things much worse for her protagonists and to start the countermove that will finally make things better. This contradictory strategy is in evidence in the first few chapters of Volume II.

Jane's bad news becomes even worse when a letter arrives from Caroline Bingley. Miss Bingley not only confirms that her brother will not be returning to Netherfield, but also ventures to predict that he will marry Miss Darcy. Three blocking figures now appear to be standing in the way of Jane's goal of a happy marriage: Darcy, Miss Bingley and now – supposedly – Darcy's sister. The evident reason why Austen is proliferating obstacles like this is to increase Jane's pain – which, in turn, will fuel Elizabeth's resentment toward Darcy when she later finds out that he is the one who has caused her sister's suffering.

But at the same time that Austen is making Jane's subplot plunge painfully lower – in order to make the Elizabeth-and-Darcy romance plummet to its mid-book low point – she is also preparing for the novel's happy ending. One of the most important ways she does this is by now introducing Elizabeth's worthy aunt and uncle, the Gardiners, who arrive "to spend the Christmas at Longbourn." The Gardiners function in the structure of the novel as antidotes to Mrs. Bennet and Lydia, as relatives who are not impediments but social assets. Early in Volume II Austen has Mrs. Gardiner invite Lizzy to a walking tour in the coming summer -- and by so doing sets up the visit to Pemberley in the beginning of Volume III.

    A change in the role that Wickham plays in the story is another important element of the countermove that Austen begins early in Volume II -- even as she prepares for the main plot's central downturn. By the time that Elizabeth is visiting Charlotte and Collins at the Parsonage, Wickham's "apparent partiality" toward Elizabeth has "subsided," since he is now pursuing Mary King -- a woman with "ten thousand pounds." Meanwhile Elizabeth has concluded that she was never actually in love with him. There seem to be two reasons why Austen separates Wickham from Elizabeth at this moment in the story. First of all, Wickham's ouster from his role as a candidate for Elizabeth's affections is a necessary preliminary to her coming change of heart toward Darcy. But an equally important reason is that, by separating Wickham from Elizabeth, Austen prepares for his later elopement with Lydia – the crisis that will lie ahead as Lydia goes off to Brighton at the end of Volume II. Austen seems to have invented Mary King solely as a stopgap, a fictional pawn to occupy Wickham during that crucial period of the plot in between his infatuation with Elizabeth and his running off with Lydia.

    The two major events that intervene during this period are Elizabeth's refusal of Darcy's proposal and her reaction to the letter he gives her the very next morning. These two consecutive mid-book events are, respectively, the main plot's nadir and the beginning of its upturn.

The main points of Darcy's letter (his defenses against the charges Elizabeth has leveled against him) initiate the unknotting of the storyline.

Darcy's first defense is against the charge that he has interfered in Jane's romance. He excuses himself, in part, by saying that he was convinced of Jane's "indifference" to Bingley – a justification that Austen has previously (Book 1, Chapter V1) gone out of her way to anticipate and make plausible by having Elizabeth reflect that the "world in general" would never suspect that Jane is "very much in love":

> " 'It may perhaps be pleasant,' replied Charlotte, 'to be able to impose on the public in such as case; but it is sometimes a disadvantage to be so guarded.' "

Clearly Charlotte's words have proved to be prophetic: Jane's guardedness has led Darcy to reach the mistaken conclusion that her heart "was not likely to be easily touched." This persuasive excuse for having separated Bingley from Jane concludes with Darcy's reason for having done it:

> "The situation of your mother's family, though objectionable, was nothing in comparison of that total want of propriety . . .."

The fact that Darcy finds the "situation" of Elizabeth's family itself "objectionable" demonstrates how much – at this point in the story – he still has in common with Lady Catherine de Bourgh. But his opinion that lower status is "nothing in comparison" to "want of propriety" anticipates how highly he will rate the Gardiners in his struggle against his pride.

The second and "more weighty accusation" that Darcy goes on to counter in his letter is "of having injured Mr. Wickham." Darcy's revelation of Wickham's "vicious propensities" is a turning point in the plot that functions both as an elucidation of a mystery and as a set-up for the crisis. The source of this mystery is the enmity between Darcy and Wickham, the reason for which Austen has previously concealed from both Elizabeth and the reader. But now Darcy's "unfolding" of Wickham's "real character" strikes Elizabeth with the force of a revelation: she sees the wrongness of her prejudice in favor of Wickham – and against Darcy. Coming immediately on the heels of her refusal of Darcy's proposal, her sudden understanding begins the upswing in the main plot's trajectory. And yet this upswing coincides with the appearance of new impediments. For Darcy's impassioned disclosure of Wickham's "want of principle" also propels the plot forward by setting the stage for the upcoming crisis – when Wickham will elope with Lydia.

Soon after Elizabeth has read Darcy's letter, she ends her stay at the Parsonage and returns with Jane to Hertfordshire. There Lydia greets them with the "excellent news" that "dear Wickham" is not going to marry Mary King. Lydia's silly exultation – and her "delicious scheme" to follow Wickham's regiment to Brighton -- are overshadowed by Elizabeth's new awareness of Wickham's iniquity. But Elizabeth can't successfully act on this awareness. She doesn't tell anyone except Jane about Wickham's depravity – and she can't persuade her father to forbid Lydia's scheme. These failures build suspense just before the crisis. For while Austen's plotting strategy in Volume II was first to bring the trajectory of the main plot to its mid-book low point and then immediately to begin its upturn, the third step of her plan was to conclude Volume II with a suspenseful conflict between hope and danger.

By the end of Volume II the conflicting opposites of the initial story problem (the contest between goals and impediments) are in equal balance. Unlike Elizabeth's blind infatuation with Wickham and Jane's misery at the end of Volume I, both sisters' prospects have brightened by end of Volume II. At last their marriage goals seem possible: Elizabeth (though she doesn't yet know it) has already begun to fall in love with Darcy; and Jane (though Elizabeth doesn't dare to tell her so) is still admired by Bingley. And yet Lydia has now emerged as a blocking figure: her "Brighton scheme" threatens to preclude her sisters' happiness. For Lydia's "total want of propriety" is just exactly what Darcy has told Elizabeth that he finds objectionable in the Bennet family. As Volume II concludes, Lydia has gone off to Brighton and Elizabeth is preparing for her trip to Pemberley. Their contradictory destinations (one sister toward Wickham and the other toward Darcy) epitomize the plot's teetering balance.

Hope seems to be winning out in the opening chapter of Volume III, when Elizabeth and the Gardiners first encounter Darcy at Pemberley. But then the news of Lydia's elopement with Wickham precipitates the sudden downturn of the crisis. This rise and fall of the storyline (like all of the ups and downs of Austen's story) is propelled by an ever-changing tension between goal-driven desire and the forces that block it.

Austen appears to have generated this tension by plotting backward, by first planning the ending of her book – where the obstacles created by the subplots are overcome in order to bring about the main plot's happy ending. For a foreknowledge of how the book would end – how the final showdown between the goal and blocking forces would be enacted – was necessary for plotting the preliminaries. Starting out with a vision of a happy ending for Elizabeth and Darcy, Austen plotted backward to prepare for it – first by positing their kind of worthy marriage as the story's goal and then, incident by incident, creating the blocking characters, inner conflicts and misjudgments that would keep her lovers apart. One obvious advantage of her technique of using three interweaving subplots to impact the main plot is the proliferation of dramatic possibilities—the opportunity for secondary characters (like Lydia, Jane, Wickham or Lady Catherine) to propel the trajectory of her protagonists either up or down. For Austen planned the interweaving of her story threads in order to create a tangle of problems that would impede her lovers from reaching their romantic understanding. But in the end all of these obstructions – the Lydia and Wickham fiasco, the bitter disagreement over Jane's romance, the ferocious pride of Lady Catherine de Bourg -- fall away like a forest of thorns.

Waugh and the Architecture of Dark Comedy

"One must have a heart of stone to read the death of little Nell without laughing."
-- Oscar Wilde

    We know (because that's what Waugh told an interviewer from *The Paris Review*) that the jungle episode in *A Handful of Dust* was the part that he wrote first. For Tony Last's comically nightmarish imprisonment by a Dickens-loving sociopath in the Amazonian rainforest is substantially the same as the fate of the cuckolded explorer in a short story entitled "The Man Who Liked Dickens." "About two years after I had written it," said Waugh, "I became interested in the circumstances which might have produced this character; in his delirium there were hints of what he might have been like in his former life, so I followed them up." *A Handful of Dust* is, then, another prime example of a novel that was plotted backwards.

    Knowing in advance that Tony's doom would be to spend the rest of his life reading Dickens aloud in a mud hut to the crazy Mr. Todd, Waugh's plot-building task was to construct the sequence of events that would bring about this final stage of Tony's torment. Seen from the vantage point of this overarching purpose, the plot of *A Handful of Dust* can be seen as having been planned to consist of two major sections: the first about Tony Last's painfully funny divorce and the second about its even funnier and more disastrous aftermath.

The post-divorce section of the novel is itself divided into three chapters: "In Search of a City," "Du Cote de Chez Todd" and "English Gothic – III." The second of these is the reworked short story about the explorer taken prisoner by the Dickens-loving madman. As an independent story in its own right, this encounter is powered by its own self-sufficient plotting mechanism. For it is a small-scale version of a familiar pattern: the conflict of antagonists.

In both the short story and the novel the initial meeting between the explorer and the madman does not appear to appear to promise any kind of conflict at all. In fact the madman (named Mr. McMaster in the story and Mr. Todd in the novel) simply seems to be offering his delirious visitor aid and comfort. In the story this initial step of the plot is followed by a flashback – telling how the explorer (named Henty) had joined a jungle expedition because his wife had confessed "her affection for another man." The flashback concludes with an account of how the only other remaining member of the expedition (named Anderson) had died of malaria, leaving Henty to wander through the jungle in a solitary delirium.

In the novel Waugh has cut out the flashback and changed the explorer's name to Tony who, in his feverish incoherence, babbles about his wife's love affair with John Beaver. But now, in both the short story and the novel, the explorer begins to recover from his illness – and Waugh begins to build a slowly mounting conflict.

The first step of this conflict coincides with the madman's first mention that he expects his visitor to read to him. This expectation --that Tony (Henty) mistakes for a pleasant request -- coincides with Mr. Todd's apparently casual statement that he has a gun. This inkling of danger is soon succeeded by something much more ominous: the grave of a black man who had read Dickens to Mr. Todd every day until he died. After Mr. Todd puts up a cross on the black man's grave ("to commemorate his death and your arrival") the conflict of wills becomes more apparent and the danger signals get louder and louder.

When Tony casually remarks that his visit will be over long before he can read every volume of Dickens, Mr. Todd's muted response suggests that Tony's readings will go on indefinitely. It is only when Tony regains his health and begins to insist upon leaving, that he notices "something slightly menacing in his host's manner." Now, step-by-step, the conflict rises. Intent upon escape, Tony tries to convince the Indians to make him a boat: but Mr. Todd will not allow them to build it.

It is at this point that the opposition of wills (covert till now) becomes suddenly overt. "Between the pages of Martin Chuzzlewit" Tony discovers a pencil-written contract: signed proof that Mr. Todd had broken his promise to release the black man from his Dickens-reading servitude. Waugh has devised this revelation in order to trigger a showdown between the antagonists. For Tony now declares that he has "read for the last time" –

and Mr. Todd counters by refusing to feed him -- a refusal reinforced by the display of a loaded gun.

    Aficionados of plot construction might by now have noticed that this pattern of rising conflict and danger is the climb up Freytag's pyramid, at the top of which there is a crisis – a decisive battle between opposites. Since poor Tony's fortunes are now decidedly at a low point, Waugh initiates the crisis by giving him a cause for hope. Waugh manufactures this hopeful upturn of Tony's story in the form of a prospector who briefly wanders through the savannah -- just long enough for Tony to slip him a note begging his friends in the outer world to rescue him. Because Tony now expects his rescuers to arrive at any moment, he feels so hopeful that he almost doesn't mind his task of reading Dickens aloud to Mr. Todd. But Tony's hope itself builds suspense in the reader's mind. For a question – "What will happen next?" – is raised by the established pattern of antagonism, the rhythm of increasingly powerful punches and counterpunches.

    Mr. Todd delivers his counterpunch – the second step of the crisis – by getting Tony to drink a soporific beverage. Tony sleeps for two days – just long enough to miss the visitors from the outer world who had finally arrived to rescue him. The hilarity of the joke depends upon its cruelty -- the fiendishly timed crushing of Tony's hopes, the ludicrous nature of his future suffering -- and upon Mr. Todd's mocking, understated sadism:

> It is a pity you missed them . . . I do not suppose we shall ever have visitors again. . ..

This final contest between Tony and Mr. Todd is the structural equivalent of James Bond's battle with the giant octopus – only here, so to speak, the octopus wins.

The incrementally unfolding calamity of Tony's encounter with Mr. Todd itself follows the crescendo of disasters in the preceding chapter of the novel, "In Search of a City." For this chapter, too, has been constructed to culminate in a sequence of progressively worsening events: the decampment of the Indian guides who leave the two explorers alone in the jungle, Tony's prostration by fever, Dr. Messinger's solitary expedition by canoe that leads to his death in a waterfall -- while Tony wanders in a delirium through the rainforest. This succession of events that get worse and worse until they build to a climax of comic awfulness (a plotting pattern that can be seen over and over again in the novel) contrasts with Tony's lifetime pursuit of a fairytale. For Tony finds himself in this predicament because he's pursuing a chimera -- a lost city on which his imagination confers the same magical allure that it has given to his beloved gothic house in England. But the romantic mirage he's been chasing after – and that has seduced him into the jungle – is in marked contrast with the life sentence of ludicrous servitude for which he's destined.

Plotting enthusiasts might find it useful to observe that this sharp contrast between a protagonist's quest and his final destination in the fiction is not at all like the plot finales we have seen in *Dr. No* and *Pride and Prejudice*. Unlike James Bond (who wants to defeat Dr. No and does) and unlike Elizabeth Bennet (who wants to marry a wonderful man with money and does), Tony Last wants a fairytale and ends up with a nightmare. This kind of ironic reversal of expectations is crucial to the plotting of dark comedy. Perhaps the most important change that Waugh made to his "The Man Who liked Dickens" story when adapting it to the novel was (after the failed quest in the jungle) to have Tony's captivity begin with his finally disillusioned recognition that "There is no City."

This is what Tony babbles to Mr. Todd when they first meet – and this first meeting, too, is an instance of Waugh's technique of ironic reversal. For the progressively worsening events of the "In Search of a City" chapter have been succeeded by the hopeful moment when Tony comes out of the jungle into the savannah where he meets the care-giving Mr. Todd. But the face of benevolent deliverance turns out to be a nightmare in disguise: Waugh has staged an apparently positive story event as a set-up for an ironic reversal. So, once again, the bottom drops out, and Tony falls down even lower.

Waugh evidently conceived of the "In Search of a City" chapter when he was in the process of adapting "The Man Who Liked Dickens" to the novel. For the long flashback that he removed from the short story (about Henty's unfaithful wife and his disastrous jungle expedition) relates many of the same events that the chapter in the novel dramatizes and expands.
But in the original short story there is no mention of the expedition's purpose: it was only when Waugh began reworking the same material for inclusion in a novel that he added the idea of a search for a lost city. By so doing

he gave his protagonist a fairytale quest that would be in keeping with Tony's daydreams about his house in the earlier part of book. Another major change that Waugh made (when he removed the flashback from the short story and used it as the plot germ for the "In Search of a City" chapter) was to change both the name and the fate of Tony's (Henty's) companion in the jungle. In the story Waugh calls him "Anderson" and kills him off by giving him malarial fever. In the novel (where his death by waterfall is much funnier) he is the unwitting herald of Tony's bad news – which is why he is called "Dr. Messinger."

    Waugh said that, in extrapolating a novel from his short story, he "followed . . .up" on the hints in Henty's delirium in order to discover the circumstances that produced him. Undoubtedly the most important of these "hints" was the unfaithful wife who appears in Henty's hallucinations as he feverishly stumbles through the jungle. This, it seems, was Waugh's first glimpse of the hideous Brenda Last, the wife and chief antagonist of his novel's diabolically tortured central character. Another major antagonist -- the wife's lover – also makes a brief appearance in the short story, but in a first draft version that is radically different from the character Waugh invented for his novel. In the short story the wife's "young man" is a "a captain in the Coldstream Guards," an exemplar of virility who is entirely unlike John Beaver – a lazy and verminous mama's boy with "school-girlish" handwriting. Curiously enough, nothing of the original iteration of the wife's lover remains in the completed novel – except the captain's name, Tony, which Waugh conferred on his hapless protagonist.

So Waugh knew in advance that Tony Last's story arc would end with him reading Dickens to a sadistically polite psychopath in the Amazonian jungle. And he knew that it had to begin with the conflict he'd hinted at in the short story – the "even-tempered, good-looking young man" versus the faithless wife and her lover. It is worth pausing over the fact that Waugh saw this conflict – the conflict of antagonists – as the essential building material of a plot. Just as he'd begun "The Man who Liked Dickens" with a first meeting of antagonists (the explorer and the madman), so he began his novel at the very moment when the story opposites start to collide.

For *A Handful of Dust* begins with the monstrous duo of Mrs. Beaver and her worthless son John discussing his upcoming weekend visit to Tony and Brenda Last. Tony has made the bad mistake of extending Beaver a casual invitation and now, like a man who has unwittingly contracted a virulent disease, he will have to pay the price. Mrs. Beaver is advising her son to seduce Tony's wife ("I should say it was time she began to be bored") – and Tony is totally unaware of the danger. Waugh has chosen to start the action of his novel at the very moment when the newly contracted disease is just about to begin its destructive work. For this is a time-honored way to begin a plot: to start when the status quo situation is first disrupted by the outbreak of a conflict, by the first sign of danger.

The story opposites – the noxious parasite and its unwitting host – are now actively engaged. And the reader suspects (although Tony doesn't) that from now on things will get worse and worse for him. In particular, the reader suspects that John Beaver will become Brenda Last's lover. So the narrative method (dramatic irony) that from now on builds suspense is fundamentally different from a mystery plot, which unfolds by uncovering unknown facts that the writer has carefully buried for the purpose of discovery. Since the danger is known in advance (in this instance that Beaver will destroy Tony's marriage) suspense is built more upon dread than upon curiosity.

Another important element of Waugh's opening gambit was to begin with Tony standing, so to speak, on an eminence: his friend Jock pronounces him to be the "happiest man I know." Waugh knew, when he began to write this novel, that he would end Tony's story by bringing him down to an opposite extreme. Tony's story arc, then, begins with him at the height of good fortune and ends with him in the depths of comic misery. As a consequence of this initial decision about the span of Tony's story arc, Waugh must have concluded that it would be necessary to create several intermediary plot points that would make Tony fall down progressively lower and lower. For this is how the sequence of events in *A Handful of Dust* does, in fact, unfold.

So like the initial chapters of *Dr. No* and of *Pride and Prejudice*, the beginning of *A Handful of Dust* introduces the novel's central conflict. In *Dr. No* the conflict is initiated by the antagonists' opening moves, by the murder of Strangways and by Bond's accepting his assignment. In *Pride and Prejudice* we see a similar pattern – where the central conflict is between the goal of a worthy marriage and the many impediments that prevent Elizabeth and Jane Bennet from reaching it. The opening chapter of *A Handful of Dust* performs a similar function by introducing the conflict and beginning the escalation of danger. But it is Brenda Last – and not John Beaver – who turns out to be Tony's major antagonist. For it is her monstrosity that drives the first and longer section of the plot. Unlike James Bond and unlike Elizabeth Bennet, Tony is not an active protagonist whose story takes the shape of a quest undertaken and finally achieved. Instead, Tony is a victim – first of Brenda's monstrosity and later of his own folly – and the spine of his story is the trajectory of his fall.

The first of the two major divisions of the novel (the part about Tony's divorce) consists of four chapters: *Du Cote de Chez Beaver*, *English Gothic*, *Hard Cheese on Tony* and *English Gothic – II*. Waugh's plotting objective, in this part of the book, was to stage an incrementally developing, excruciatingly slow disaster. The proliferation of ridiculous characters and situations relieves the reader's suffering, so that poor Tony slides down on a knife's edge between pain and laughter.

While the first chapter of the novel introduces the conflict, John Beaver's imminent attack upon Tony Last's marriage, the second chapter (*English Gothic*) is a step-by-step relation of its growth – and of the early stages of Tony's torture. The curtain rises on the weekend when Brenda Last and John Beaver first meet -- and when Tony and Brenda's little boy (also very purposely named John) first appears onstage. Now the drama of Tony's cuckoldry begins as Brenda decides to take a flat in London. After this initial step, things get worse and worse for Tony: Beaver takes Brenda to a party; they kiss in a taxi; the newly rented flat becomes their love nest, and their affair becomes the talk of London society. The chapter's worsening sequence of incidents builds to a culminating event that makes the marital rift even wider: Brenda tells Tony that she's "living" at the flat – in order to take a supposed course in "economics."

At the beginning of *Hard Cheese on Tony*, Tony has already taken to drink. Desperate yet unsuspecting, he has come to London to see Brenda. But he never gets to see her. Instead, he and his friend Jock get soused on Burgundy, go to a seedy nightclub and pester Brenda with their drunken phone calls. Feeling guilty for his disgraceful behavior, Tony – even more miserable than before -- goes back to his Gothic manor house and eagerly awaits Brenda's return.

But Tony's pathetic eagerness is only a set-up for another one of Waugh's ironic reversals. For when Brenda does finally come home, she is accompanied by an entourage of derisive females – including John Beaver's mother, who wants to cover the walls of Tony's beloved house with "white chromium plating." Up to this point Waugh has designed the sequence of Brenda's actions and words so that they build in a crescendo of monstrosity. As her monstrosity increases, Waugh intensifies the pain by simultaneously revealing Tony's total blindness. Now she tries to "get him interested in a girl" -- a scheme she devises in order to keep him from drinking, which she would prefer to prevent because it would "make everything very difficult" for her. It is only when this attempt fails (and when everyone – except Tony – knows about Brenda's affair with John Beaver) that the time for the annual foxhunt finally arrives. It is now that Brenda and Tony's obnoxious, horse-jumping little boy (the other John in the story) takes center stage. Predictably, he dies -- in a hunting accident.

    Little John Andrew's death is predictable because Waugh has gone out of his way, since the beginning of the novel, to let the reader know that it is going to happen. Again and again Waugh has let it be known (through the repeated warnings of a fretful nanny, for example) that something very bad was going to happen as a result of the little boy's dangerous horsemanship. Although just exactly how little John Andrew will die is unknown, the reader has known since the opening pages of the second chapter that the fact of it is certain. Waugh's suspense-building method here (like the predicted danger to Tony's marriage in the first chapter of the novel) is dramatic irony – and the expectation of the little boy's death, added to the worsening pain of Tony's marriage, compounds the dread of the coming calamity. But Waugh's proliferation of ludicrous characters and devilish plot turns – together with the fact that the little boy is himself so unappealing – turns the expectation of his death into an excruciating joke. The reader, in between painful dread and laughter, turns the page.

So little John Andrew's death – a major plot point situated midway in the novel – does not come as a surprise. But it ratchets up Tony's pain and fuels the ensuing build-up of suspense. For now the focus of Tony's agony – and of the reader's curiosity – is on what Brenda's reaction to her little boy's death will be. Expectant tension builds as Tony stays at home, while he sends his friend Jock to London to tell Brenda what has happened. It is during this expectant interval that the ironic gulf between Brenda's monstrosity and Tony's good-natured blindness is stretched to its widest extreme. "It's going to be so much worse for Brenda," says Tony. "You see she's got nothing else, much, except John . . . you see, I know Brenda so well." It is the pent-up tension of this interval that powers the drama of its release – the words that Brenda speaks when at last she finds out that her little boy is dead: "John . . . John Andrew . . . I . . . Oh thank God . . ."

These seven words are the dramatic apogee of the four-chapter-long divorce section of the novel: when Brenda utters them, they function like the punch-line of an elaborate and cruel joke. For now the reader understands why Waugh has given the same name – John – both to Brenda's little boy and to her lover. All day long Brenda has been worrying that her lover – John Beaver – might have had an accident. So when Jock tells her that "John" is dead, she at first thinks that Beaver has died. A moment later, Brenda learns otherwise – and is greatly relieved to learn that, instead, it is merely her little boy who is dead. As the single most important turning point in the plot, this appalling revelation functions in a number of very different ways.

On the one hand it is a revelation for the reader – who now fully understands what a monster Brenda really is. But from Brenda's point of view it is an altogether different kind of epiphany. For, as she later tells Beaver: "Until Wednesday, when I thought something had happened to you, I had no idea that I loved you." This realization, in turn, precipitates Brenda's big decision – to divorce Tony and marry John Beaver. So the dramatic climax when Brenda learns that it is her son and not her lover who has died is the tipping point for Tony and Brenda – the decisive moment between the antagonists of the drama. It is, in other words, the crisis – the top of Freytag's pyramid. It is the dramatic event which all of the preceding incidents of the plot build up to and from which all of the succeeding incidents fall.

Waugh has also designed this major turning point of the plot so that it is a revelation about Jock – the friend whom Tony has sent to London to tell Brenda about little John Andrew's death. Jock is the only one who hears Brenda's words ("Oh thank God") and so is the only witness to her surpassing monstrosity. "You know what you said," he tells her later. And yet at the end of the book (after Beaver has jilted Brenda and after Tony is presumed to be dead) Jock marries Brenda. What kind of man would want to marry such a monster?

Waugh planned *Hard Cheese on Tony* so that its culminating drama would depend upon a sequence of plot points that lead one to another like a succession of falling dominoes. He planned little John Andrew's death so that it would trigger the crisis, the moment when Brenda's relieved reaction to the news of her little boy's death makes her decide to divorce Tony and to marry John Beaver. This transformative event in turn brings about the chapter's final dramatic moment – when Tony reads Brenda's letter informing him of her decision. So the chapter ends with another event that suddenly changes everything – when Tony's ignorance at last gives way to horrified disbelief. "But it's not true, is it?" he asks. "Yes, I'm afraid it is," says Jock: "Everyone has known for some time."

This causal sequence of dramatic events is another bit of evidence that the way a completed plot unfolds is a very different thing from the logical order of plot construction. The crisis of the plot, for example, depends upon Waugh's having given the same name – John – both to Brenda's lover and to her little boy. But Waugh must have decided to do this (and to kill off the little boy) before he composed his first chapter. Otherwise, why – in the novel's opening chapter – does he have Mrs. Beaver tell her son (John) that Tony and Brenda have "one child at least, perhaps more"? Otherwise why does he give so much onstage time in the preliminary chapters of the book to the little boy (John) and his pony? Although the crisis of the plot (when Brenda learns that her little boy is dead) doesn't occur until the middle of the novel, Waugh must have designed it early on – and then plotted backwards to create the succession of events that would lead up to it.

But from what Waugh said (in his *Paris Review* interview) about following up on "hints" in his short story in order to find the beginnings of a novel, it would appear that his very earliest plotting decisions were about establishing a conflict of antagonists -- the "even-tempered" young man versus the adulterous wife and her lover. It seems at least quite likely that a second step would have been to figure out the mechanism of the crisis. It must have been evident to Waugh from the outset that this crisis would have to bring about the breakdown of his protagonist's marriage: for the short story straightforwardly states that the protagonist's decision to join an expedition to the Amazon was a consequence of his wife's "confessing her affection for another man." But when Waugh started building the plot of his novel, he apparently discovered that he needed something more shocking than the prosaic adultery of the short story as a mechanism for triggering a crisis. The fact that his antagonists were to be a husband and a wife suggested that a child might also be involved: Waugh's penchant for horrible – and yet comic -- events led him ineluctably to the conclusion that this child would somehow have to die.

In his *Paris Review* interview Waugh said that there are two kinds of fictional characters: "There are the protagonists and there are characters who are furniture." Apparently Waugh designed his protagonists first -- Tony and Brenda Last -- and then the "furniture" came into being as a result of these initial creations. Their little boy, John Andrew, is the novel's most important piece of "furniture" -- who came into being as a result of Waugh's need to build a shocking crisis that would reveal Brenda Last's fundamental perversity. Once the death of this child – and the confusion of names with the wife's lover – were part of Waugh's story design, then other minor characters (like the child's nanny and the farmhand who teaches him how to ride) were born as a consequence.

Mrs. Beaver, John Beaver's mother, is another interesting example of a character – a piece of furniture – coming into being as a direct consequence of Waugh's initial choice of a central conflict for the divorce section of the novel. We know that the process by which Waugh arrived at this choice began with the conflict in his short story – where the husband decides to join an expedition to the Amazon because his wife has taken a lover. Somewhere in the process of transforming this germinal idea into a conflict strong enough to power a novel, he decided that the wife would be -- not just the chief antagonist – but a pretty and deceitful monster. This decision, in turn, led to the conclusion that this pretty monster's choice of a lover would necessarily be perverse. It must have been through a process of thought something like this that the lazy, selfish, utterly unprincipled mama's boy – John Beaver – slithered into being. His hideously opportunistic Mother – whose creature he entirely is—must have emerged at the same time as a necessary adjunct.

So secondary characters like little John Andrew and Mrs. Beaver seem to have come into being as a direct consequence of Waugh's first and fundamental decision – the choice of a conflict and the design of his antagonists. His initial decision to cast the wife in his domestic drama as a "vixen" unleashed the process of thought that led to Brenda Last's indifference to her child's death and to her obsession with a verminous mama's boy. In order to power his plot's unfolding of ironic events, Waugh designed his other antagonist – Tony Last – to be Brenda's diametrical opposite: an honorable and gullible schlemiel. By yoking these opposing characters together Waugh established a dynamic to drive his comedy of pain.

The last chapter of the divorce section of the novel, *English Gothic –II*, is the bridge between the crisis in Tony's marriage and his disastrous jungle expedition. So it functions both as what is commonly called the "falling action" of the divorce drama (the post-crisis descent down the right-hand side of Freytag's pyramid) and as a set-up for the comically awful jungle episode that is to follow. As a wrap-up of the first major section of the novel, this chapter concludes the preceding drama by playing out the farce of Tony's divorce. But at the same time it sets the stage for Tony's final plunge. For it presents him – not just as Brenda's victim – but as his own victim as well, a blindly decent stooge always supremely capable of shooting himself in the foot.

Because it is the gentlemanly thing to do (and because he is a jackass) Tony agrees that Brenda should play the part of the "innocent and injured party" and he of the adulterous cad in their divorce proceedings. Tony's asinine willingness to submit to this arrangement fuels the comedy of the next segment of the plot – his staged adultery with a floozy at a Brighton hotel. Tony's blind decency also leads him to suppose that Brenda will honor a previous agreement to a modest divorce settlement: "Lady Brenda's word is quite good enough," he says. This high-mindedly stupid declaration (in the first few pages of the chapter) is the set-up for the pratfall of the chapter's final scene– in which Brenda's fat, grave-desecrating brother demands that Tony pay her an exorbitant alimony.

The comedy of both of these episodes (Tony's staged adultery with Milly and his showdown with Reggie St. Cloud) depends upon the technique of ironic reversal. Evidently Tony's staged adultery -- his pretending to be a philandering husband while Brenda gets to play the injured wife -- is funny because it enacts the exact opposite of the painful facts. And it is all the funnier because Tony's ludicrous code of chivalry seems to require it. The point here that those of us who make up stories shouldn't miss is that this ironic plotting is a direct consequence of Waugh's prior and fundamental choice of a fictional conflict – specifically his initial decision to design his married antagonists as diametrically and comically opposite character types. For the understanding that Brenda will always be a pretty monster and that Tony will always be a decent dupe is the ongoing ironic joke underneath all -- but one -- of the story events that involve their interaction.

The one exception to this comic pattern is the very last event of the chapter (and of the divorce section of the novel as a whole). For when Brenda's brother demands a staggering alimony, Tony flatly refuses: "I am going away for six months or so. When I come back, if she wishes it, I shall divorce Brenda without settlements of any kind." Up until this culminating plot twist, Tony's trajectory has consistently fallen lower and lower: but here it turns momentarily upward. So Waugh punctuates Tony's agonizing, four-chapter-long downfall with a surprisingly hopeful plot twist which appears to suggest that Tony has finally discovered a backbone and wakened from his daydreams. But Tony, of course, is wrong: he is not coming back after six months. Instead will live out the rest of his life in a mud hut reading Dickens aloud to Mr. Todd. Nor has he truly wakened from his romantic daydreams. Instead, he will substitute his fantasies about his Gothic castle with a fool's quest for a lost city in the jungle. So Tony's apparently hopeful moment of strength and clarity is another example of one of Waugh's recurrent plotting techniques: the ironic set-up – a springboard for the nosedive that is to follow.

    Tony's increasingly disastrous jungle expedition is cross-cut by a succession of very brief scenes that show what Brenda, Jock and Beaver are simultaneously doing back in London. When he is lying in his hammock and scratching insect bites, for example, Tony falls asleep -- and the scene suddenly shifts to a party in London at which Brenda is dancing with Jock. The divorce plot and the jungle expedition plot are otherwise two independent storylines: but this cinematic cross-cutting ties the two plotlines together.

    Waugh reinforces the interconnection between these two plotlines by making Tony's fortunes in the jungle and Brenda's fortunes back at home get progressively worse in tandem. For Tony reaches the verge of calamity at the very moment when Brenda's affair with Beaver begins to fall apart: just when Tony reaches the border of the region in which he will be taken prisoner by Mr. Todd, his storyline is cross-cut by a scene in which Mrs. Beaver persuades her son John to go away with her to America. A later episode in which Tony and Dr. Messinger are abandoned in the jungle by their Indian guides is cross-cut by a similar scene of abandonment -- in which Beaver tells Brenda that he is going away to America, and Brenda can't persuade him to do otherwise. An even worse set-back for Tony (Dr. Messinger's death, that leaves him all alone and sick with fever in the jungle) is cross-cut by a parallel set-back for Brenda: an unsuccessful attempt to get money from Tony's solicitor. This sequence of cross-cuts between Tony's and Brenda's storylines concludes when each falls to an even lower depth of misery. Tony is lying in his hammock in the jungle, crying periodically, beset by feverish hallucinations. Meanwhile, back in London, Brenda is all alone and in "an agony of resentment and self-pity." Beaver has arrived in America, and her affair with him is over.

But now, just when Tony reaches the savannah where he encounters the Dickens-loving Mr. Todd, this parity of falling fortunes comes to an end. Tony's fortunes, of course, will fall even further. But Brenda's star will rise again – a plotting surprise that Waugh reserved for the novel's final chapter.

The last chapter of the novel, "English Gothic – III," takes place on the day when the heirs to Tony's Gothic castle unveil a memorial in Tony's honor. This unveiling is the final twist in Tony's plot-line and the supposed solemnity of the event (and of his being remembered as an "Explorer") is undercut by mocking irony. For one thing, Tony isn't dead at all – but alive in Brazil reading Dickens to Mr. Todd: this is the ridiculous hell to which Tony's daydreams of exploration have enticed him. The fact that Beaver's mother ("one of Tony's closest friends") has suggested the memorial adds one more note of sardonic irony.

But it is Brenda and Jock who inflict Tony's final indignity. For Brenda is much too busy to attend Tony's unveiling – instead she has to be with Jock, Tony's supposed best friend and her new husband. This comically nasty turn of events concludes the ironic dynamic between Brenda and Tony: Brenda's final good fortune is one last kick in the pants for Tony.

In order to construct this final, ironic twist of the plot, Waugh needed to improvise a way to make Brenda and her socially acceptable monstrosity triumph the end of his novel. It was evidently for this reason that Jock Grant Menzies -- another of Waugh's pieces of fictional "furniture" ---came into being. For Jock's primary function in the plot (which Waugh somewhat disguises by casting Jock as Tony's pal and by giving Jock a girl friend) is to marry Brenda at the end of the novel -- after Tony is presumed to be dead and after Beaver has jilted her. Jock's major purpose as a character, in other words, is to provide the crucial upturn to the end of Brenda's storyline – to show that her fortunes have risen at the same time that Tony's have miserably plummeted. So (from the very first chapter) Waugh worked Jock into his plot in order to prepare for the novel's final irony.

Waugh designed the last chapter of his novel so that these final twists in Tony's and Brenda's storylines would be merely incidental events in the life of the family who are now the heirs to Tony's "Gothic" castle. Tony's unveiling and Brenda's remarriage are now relegated to the background, while the foreground is occupied by this family whose present doings initiate an entirely new plotline projected forward into an unfolding future. The result of this radical shifting of perspective is analogous to the cinematic use of the wide-angle shot, the camera's drawing back from a close-up to take in a broader prospect.

For the narrative focus now expands beyond Tony and Brenda to include the perpetuation of the upper-crust society to which they belong. Indeed the preservation of this privileged caste appears to be the one thing that Tony's successors care about: their driving purpose is to restore his Gothic castle – and so carry on his supposedly glorious tradition – by raising silver foxes.

It soon becomes apparent that making a profit from silver foxes is a cruel and murderous business. For although they are beautiful, foxes are nasty, biting little animals -- and Tony's heirs "can't shoot enough" rabbits to keep them fed. The abbreviated plotline that Waugh invented for this epilogue to his novel highlights this blithe slaughtering of rabbits for the feeding of greedy foxes. Waugh especially emphasizes the cruelty of this sacrifice by dramatizing it in the novel's humorously grisly last scene – where one of Tony's heirs is seen bringing in fresh bundles of dead rabbits ("skinned and tied round the feet") while the eager foxes "run up to the doors" of their cages. Waugh evidently designed this final moment of the novel's plot as a darkly satiric re-enactment of the cruel dynamics of Tony-and-Brenda's story.

He makes this quite obvious by drawing a broad parallel between a "little vixen" who has had her "brush bitten off" and Brenda who has likewise had her bitter dose of suffering. But now, just like this vicious creature, Brenda is "little the worse for her accident." While the vicious foxes we see in the novel's final scene are plainly fictional proxies for Brenda, the dead rabbits they are just about to rip apart are evidently just like poor Tony. But this gruesome final beat of the novel's plot does much more than sum up the dynamics between Tony and Brenda. For it doesn't only look backward to the events of the preceding story. It also looks forward and so suggests something even darker -- that this sacrifice of rabbits to vicious foxes will happen over and over and over again in the as-yet-unseen future.

At first glance it would seem like we are far away from the nightmare world of the vampire novel. But in fact – compared with the triumphant monsters in Waugh's *A Handful of Dust* -- Bram Stoker's *Dracula* is a pleasant dream. For at the end of Stoker's novel the blood-sucking fiend has been killed: the forces of light – Van Helsing and the bland society of Jonathan and Mina

Harker and their friends – have vanquished the powers of darkness. Stoker, in other words, dispels the horrors of his tale by resorting to the most comforting convention in the story-maker's arsenal: the vision of order restored. Order is also restored in the final chapter of *A Handful of Dust*: another upper-crust, fox-hunting family has succeeded to Tony Last's gothic manor house at Hetton. But the order that Tony's heirs perpetuate is itself covertly monstrous.

Conflict and the Logic of Story-building

"We have seen that a play consists, or ought to consist, of a great crisis, worked out through a series of minor crises."
 -- William Archer, *Play-Making: A Manual of Craftsmanship*

These three novels – *Dr. No*, *Pride and Prejudice* and *A Handful of Dust* -- are obviously quite different. Yet there is one striking similarity that they share: each is, fundamentally, the story of a conflict. In Ian Fleming's novel the conflict is between James Bond and Dr. No. In *Pride and Prejudice* the conflict is between the Bennet sisters' goal of a worthy marriage and the various impediments that, until the very end of the book, keep them from achieving it. In *A Handful of Dust* the plot is driven forward by Tony Last's conflict with his chief tormentors – Brenda, John Beaver and the Dicken-loving Mr. Todd. In each of these three books the plot points – the important moments of dramatic change—are stages in the life cycle of the central conflict.

In each novel it is the characterization of the antagonists that governs the design of the conflict – and of the plot points that comprise it. And in each book the plot is structured to introduce, increase and finally resolve conflict: each book, in other words, takes the shape of Freytag's pyramid.

The plot of each book begins with the presentation of a story problem – a turn of events that triggers a conflict and introduces the clash of the antagonists. In *Dr. No* this triggering mechanism is a sequence of action and reaction: the double murder of Strangways and Mary Trueblood, followed by James Bond's assignment to investigate their disappearance. In *Pride and Prejudice* the mechanism that triggers the story is fundamentally the same: a conflict is introduced and the battle between the antagonists begins. Here, of course, the conflict is not a face-off between a mysterious arch-villain and a heroic secret agent, but a predicament that the Bennet sisters face because their marriage goal is obstructed by the "low" behavior and negligible fortune of their family. In the opening chapter of the novel (where the marriage goal and the foolish Mrs. Bennet are juxtaposed) Austen plants the seeds of the conflict. By the time Elizabeth and Jane first meet Darcy and Bingley at a dance, this potential problem has become an open battle. For now the chief antagonists are both onstage and the "low" behavior of the Bennet family is on a collision course with Darcy's pride -- a conflict that Elizabeth's prejudice will soon make worse. The triggering of the conflict in *A Handful of Dust* follows the same basic pattern. Here the conflict is the breakdown of Tony Last's marriage and the event that triggers it is a casual invitation: Tony asks John Beaver to visit him and Brenda for the weekend. Immediately the antagonists are set at odds: first when Beaver's discussion with his mother maps out their campaign against Tony, and then as Beaver's first meeting with Brenda begins the assault upon Tony's happiness.

The opening gambits of all three novels – each of which begins a conflict and introduces the antagonists – in one way or another sound the note of danger. The kind of danger in each book is unique to each specific conflict. In the James Bond thriller (where the conflict is against an entirely external antagonist) the danger is completely physical – the threat of pain and death. The double murder in the opening sequence of the novel immediately sounds the alarm. In *Pride and Prejudice* (where Darcy struggles against his pride while Elizabeth contends with her prejudice) the conflict is internal – and the dangers are of the heart. At the first dance, when Elizabeth meets Darcy and Bingley meets Jane, the happiness of both couples is already at stake. The danger that at first threatens and later ravages Tony Last in *A Handful of Dust* is also a suffering of the heart. But unlike Elizabeth Bennet's affecting and exclusively emotional pain, Tony's hilarious suffering comes to include physical torment and a brush with death. From the novel's very first chapter, when Beaver and his mother conspire against him, Tony is already in danger.

In each of these novels the danger is the felt response to the conflict and so is inseparable from it and from the introduction of the antagonists. It is this initial danger (the threat to James Bond, the emotional peril that the Bennet sisters and Tony Last all face) that forges the sympathetic bond with the reader. The danger is the bait on the hook.

Once this hook has been planted by each novel's opening sequence, the major purpose of each plot is to provide more and more danger until the conflict reaches a crisis. In Ian Fleming's novel the danger mounts, step by step: a beautiful Chinese girl attacks Quarrel with a broken flashbulb; someone leaves poisoned fruit and a deadly centipede in Bond's hotel room; two look-alikes Bond has hired to impersonate him and Quarrel are murdered; Quarrel gets burned to death by a mechanical, fire-breathing Dragon just before Bond gets captured and tortured. Each event ratchets up the danger as James Bond gets closer and closer to the showdown with his enemy. As different as *Pride and Prejudice* is from *Dr. No*, this pattern of increasing peril is the same. The introduction of the central conflict is followed by a succession of major story events that Austen designed in order to make the initial problem progressively worse. Austen accomplishes this primarily by creating a number of blocking figures who generate complications in the interweaving subplots.

In the first half of the novel the most important of these blocking figures is Mrs. Bennet, who epitomizes the "low" behavior that gets in the way of the Bennet sisters' marriage goals. As a blocking figure Mrs. Bennet's major function is to bring about a head-on collision with Darcy's pride and so endanger Jane's romance with Bingley. This complication in Jane's subplot in turn brings about the major reversal in the main plot – when, in the very middle of the novel, Elizabeth learns of Darcy's injury to her sister and so refuses to marry him. Other blocking figures -- like

Lydia, Wickham and Lady Catherine de Bourg – serve a similar function: to increase conflict and in so doing build suspenseful danger.

This same pattern -- a succession of story events that progressively build danger and suspense – is also evident in the way Waugh builds his plot in *A Handful of Dust*. The danger to Tony's happiness gets worse and worse as, incident-by-incident, Beaver and Brenda become more and more intimate. Their affair starts out merely as a casual conversation on the weekend when they meet. But when Brenda rents a flat in London and Beaver takes her to a party, their involvement – and the threat to Tony's marriage – becomes somewhat more serious. When Beaver kisses Brenda in a taxi, the danger level crosses into the red zone. The story event that concludes the second chapter – Brenda's announcement that she will be living at the flat in order to take a course in "economics" – pulls apart Tony's marriage to the breaking point.

This series of incrementally worsening incidents eventually culminates in a catastrophic turn of events – little John Andrew's death – a plot point that is the structural equivalent of Elizabeth Bennet's refusal of Darcy's marriage proposal at the midpoint of *Pride and Prejudice*. For just as Austen invented Darcy's interference in Jane's romance in order to set off a chain reaction of events that would bring about the main plot's major reversal, so Waugh invented little John Andrew for the sole purpose of making his death become a pivotal disaster half-way through the novel. It is for exactly the same reason -- in order to lay the groundwork for a major reversal -- that Fleming makes Quarrel so prominent in his story. Quarrel's death (like the death of little John Andrew and like Elizabeth's rejection of Darcy's proposal) is the climax of a sequence of increasing dangers. Each one of these black moments precedes and prepares for the crisis.

Each of these dark turning points is, of course, tailor-made to fit a particular central conflict and the characterization of particular antagonists. When the central conflict is an entirely external battle between a heroic secret agent and a mysterious and sadistic villain, the black moment comes when a mechanical, fire-breathing "dragon" burns a buddy to death. When the battleground is the heart and the antagonists are a young woman blinded by her prejudice and a young man struggling with his pride, her refusal to marry him is the most painful moment. When the battleground is a marriage and the antagonists are a clueless stooge and a heartless beauty, the nadir is the death of their little boy.

Each one of these major reversals -- each pinnacle of danger and suspense – prepares for a crisis in its own unique way. In the Ian Fleming novel Quarrel's grisly death brings the drama to a height of expectant tension: the curious reader turns the page in order to see what greater dangers lie ahead when James Bond finally does battle with his enemy. In the Austen novel Elizabeth's refusal to marry Darcy impels him to resolve the crisis when Lydia runs off with Wickham. And so the lovers' darkest moment leads directly to their transformation – the overcoming of Darcy's pride and the overturning of Elizabeth's prejudice. In *A Handful of Dust* the major reversal similarly leads to the crisis and to the transformation of the antagonists. Like a succession of falling dominos, one event precipitates the next: the little boy's death triggers Brenda's realization that she loves John Beaver – which in turn shatters Tony's marriage.

The central conflict presented at the beginning of each one of these novels comes to a head at the crisis. In other words, the plot's overture and its crisis are inseparable: whereas the overture starts a conflict and makes the reader question how it will end, the crisis decides the conflict and so provides an answer to this question. In Ian Fleming's novel the conflict begins immediately – when Strangways' murder sets Bond on a collision course with Dr. No. The question about how this conflict will turn out is answered at the crisis – when James Bond decisively wins his battle with the giant squid. We see the same interconnection – between the question asked by the overture and the answer provided by the crisis – in *Pride and Prejudice*. Here, once again, the introductory chapters present a central conflict that poses an implicit question – whether or not the Bennet sisters' marriage objectives will be thwarted by their family's low behavior and negligible fortune. This conflict between marriage and family reaches a crisis when Lydia runs off with Wickham: for this is the greatest possible challenge to Darcy's pride and therefore the greatest threat to the sisters' prospects. When Darcy chooses love over pride, he decides the conflict and so answers the question that had been raised when the conflict was first introduced. In Waugh's novel, too, the crisis decides a conflict and so answers a question that this conflict has raised in the reader's mind. Here the conflict is between Tony, on the one hand, and Brenda and Beaver on the other. Since the reader has guessed, since the first page of the novel, that things were not going to go well for Tony, the question has never been who was going to win this battle. The question, instead, has been: "How will Tony get screwed?" The answer to this question comes when the conflict builds to a critical moment of choice: when the death of Tony and Brenda's child becomes the catalyst for Brenda's decision – to divorce Tony and marry Beaver instead.

While the plots of all three of these novels start out by introducing a conflict that in one way or another sounds the note of danger – and then proceed to increase this danger at first incrementally and then exponentially until the crisis decides the conflict, the basic purpose of their plots immediately after the crisis is to reverse this process by decreasing the danger as the conflict winds down. This entire plotting process – cranking up a dangerous conflict, bringing it to a crisis and then uncranking it -- is, of course, the climb up and down Freytag's pyramid. The second half of this process -- the climb down the pyramid -- is succinctly carried out by the concluding episodes of *Dr. No*. Here the crisis (Bond's battle with the squid) immediately leads to the climax (the death of Dr. No) – which in turn immediately leads to the end of the book, Bond's romantic interlude with Honey. In *Pride and Prejudice* the climb down the pyramid is accomplished by means of a cascade of major turning points in the three subplots. First Darcy resolves the crisis that had been ignited when Lydia ran off with Wickham. Then he retracts his earlier objection to Bingley's marriage with Jane. Lastly, he defies his prideful aunt, Lady Catherine de Bourg. The complications in each one of these subplots (Wickham's, Jane's and Lady Catherine's) had previously served the story-building purpose of keeping Elizabeth and Darcy apart. So the unknotting of these subplots in turn unknots the main plot – and brings Elizabeth and Darcy together

In *A Handful of Dust* the story events immediately after the crisis are also – at least apparently – devoted to winding down the conflict and wrapping things up. After he has learned that Brenda will divorce him and marry Beaver instead, Tony's climb down the pyramid consists of two episodes in which he contends with the aftermath of his loss. In the first, he submits to the farce of a staged adultery. In the second, he defies his pompous brother-in-law, telling him that he refuses to pay Brenda an exorbitant alimony. But Tony's sudden discovery of a backbone and his announcement that he is "going away for six months or so" are misleading indications that he has landed on his feet. Instead, a trapdoor opens and he falls down even farther -- into the Amazon jungle in the last part of the book.

Once Tony lands in the Amazon, the same pyramidal plotting pattern (in which a dangerous conflict mounts step-by-step to a crisis and then subsides) is repeated: not once, but twice. In the first of these mini-dramas Waugh has once again set up a conflict: Tony and Dr. Messinger are the protagonists – and their antagonist is the jungle itself. Danger mounts by degrees: first their Indian guides abandon them, and then things get even worse when Tony develops a fever – and then becomes delirious. The crisis of this episode (the moment of decisive battle with the jungle) comes when Dr. Messenger goes off alone in his canoe in order to look for help – but ends up tumbling down a waterfall and drowning. After this, the episode draws to a close (and the conflict subsides) as Tony, still delirious, finally stumbles out of the jungle – and reaches the false safety of Mr. Todd's hut.

But it is now that another trapdoor opens and a second pyramidal conflict begins. Here Tony's antagonist is Mr. Todd: once again, the danger of conflict rises step-by-step by means of a progression of worsening story events. The first two of these events make it clear that Tony is in danger: Mr. Todd casually mentions that he has a gun and later shows Tony the grave of a black man who had read aloud to him every day until he died. The antagonism – and the danger level – soon rise one step higher: when Tony insists upon leaving, Mr. Todd becomes "slightly menacing." But when Tony discovers a contract – signed proof that Mr. Todd had broken his promise to release the black man from his servitude – the danger of the conflict jumps nearly to the top of the pyramid. Now Tony's attempts to escape – followed by Mr. Todd's counter-maneuvers – build in animosity like an exchange of punches that culminate in a knockout. When Tony finally manages to get word to his friends in the outer world, Mr. Todd lands the final punch – by drugging Tony so that he is sound asleep until long after the rescue party has decided that he is dead and gone away. Because Tony has now decisively lost another battle, Mr. Todd's final and hilarious imperative ("Let us read little Dorrit again.") brings the plot to the bottom of the pyramid and the end of the conflict.

While the openings of these three novels introduce a central conflict, their final chapters serve the diametrically opposite function of bringing the central conflict to a close. In other words, the two bases of Freytag's pyramid – on the left and right – are mirror images of one another. In the Ian Fleming novel the final chapter (in which Bond and Honey make love) is a modern variant of the time-honored plot device of ending a discord with a marriage. Like the royal wooing in the last act of Shakespeare's *Henry V*, Bond and Honey's lovemaking reverses the dynamic of conflict that opened the story. Obviously the multiple marriages that conclude *Pride and Prejudice* serve the same function. But the last chapter of *A Handful of Dust* puts an end to Tony's troubles with an ironic travesty of closure. For here all of the social conventions that suggest a dignified resolution of the past (Brenda's remarriage, the unveiling of Tony's monument, the succession of Tony's heirs to his gothic castle) only mask the perpetuation of folly and viciousness.

The pyramidal pattern in each of these novels (the way their plots have been designed as a consecutive series of incidents that introduce a conflict, build it to a crisis and finally bring it to closure) should not be confused with the logical order of construction – the sequence of steps their creators took as they went about the process of improvising incidents and characters before assembling them in their final form. In other words, the order of incidents in a completed plot – arranged from the beginning to the end of the story -- is not necessarily the same as the order of their creation. For example, we know as a fact (because Waugh said so) that he plotted his novel in reverse – starting with a short story that is now the chapter at the end of the book about Tony's encounter with Mr. Todd and only then inventing all the preceding incidents about Tony's marriage with Brenda. A careful consideration of the plot of *Pride and Prejudice* supports a similar hypothesis: that Austen first planned the novel's denouement and only then plotted the incidents that would lead up to it. It is obvious, too, that the completed plot of *Dr. No* – the sequence of incidents – should not be mistaken for the sequence of steps Fleming took in order to build a plot: Fleming did not write *Dr. No* until he had already built a carefully structured storyline. The completed plot of Dr. No is itself *de facto* proof of this. For example, Quarrel's role in the story -- the way Fleming builds his importance only in order to make his death a major turning point -- is evidence of planning in advance. Other story elements that are casually mentioned early on and later prove to be crucial to the plot – like the fire-breathing dragon and the giant squid – are more persuasive evidence of a carefully premeditated storyline.

So if these three novelists – Ian Fleming, Jane Austen and Evelyn Waugh – did not just blindly begin on page one and grope their way to a plot, what did they do? If — instead of flying blind -- they did not start to write until they already had at least the broad outline of a story, how had they begun to build this structure? The answer to this question lies on every page of these three novels -- in plain view, just like the "purloined letter" in Poe's tale. For each one of the moments of dramatic change in each one of these novels – each of the so-called "plot points" – is a stage in the evolution of a central conflict: each incident serves either to introduce the conflict, increase the conflict, bring it to a crisis or give it closure. Therefore it must have been an initial decision about the conflict itself – what it would be and who the antagonists were – that was the very first step in the plotting process.

This becomes evident when we take a look at a major incident in each of these novels. Think, for example, of the scene in *Dr. No* where the young Chinese woman slashes Quarrel's face with a broken flashbulb. This incident is evidently an important turning point in the conflict between Bond and Dr. No – the moment when the dangerous conflict escalates from threats to physical injury. This plot point is a corollary – a logical consequence – of what must have been Fleming's primary decision about the kind of book he was going to write: that his novel's structure would be built upon the conflict between Bond and Dr. No – and that Dr. No would be a mysterious villain. This initial decision to make his villain mysterious in turn resulted in more decisions: to keep his villain offstage for as long as possible, which meant that it would be necessary to invent evil surrogates who would threaten Bond until the evil mastermind finally appeared. So the young Chinese woman who slashes Quarrel's face with a broken flashbulb is a secondary character who came into being as consequence of prior and more fundamental decisions that Fleming had made about the structure of his plot.

Now consider an incident in *Pride and Prejudice*: the scene at the Netherfield ball where Mrs. Bennet's foolish and "low" behavior makes Darcy decide to persuade his friend Bingley not to marry Jane. Like the scene in *Dr. No* where the young Chinese woman slashes Quarrel's face, this incident is the major turning point when the level of the conflict rises from threatened harm to outright danger. This scene where Darcy and Mrs. Bennet collide is the first skirmish of the novel's central conflict – the conflict that the Bennet sisters struggle with because their hopes to be well married are threatened by their family's indiscretion and inadequate fortune. Evidently, Austen conceived of this crucial plot point -- just as she designed all of the other steps of the conflict -- only after she had first decided what the central conflict and who her antagonists would be.

The analogous plot point in *A Handful of Dust* – the incident when the level of the conflict escalates from potential to actual danger – is the moment when Beaver and Brenda kiss in a taxi. Like all of the other turning points of the story, this incident is a step of the conflict between Tony and his tormentors – and a logical consequence of Waugh's initial plotting decisions: his choice of a conflict and of the antagonists who would enact it. In fact we do know (from what Waugh said in his *Paris Review* interview) that this was indeed how he began to plot his novel. For the "hints" in his short story that he "followed . . . up" were suggestions about a marital conflict – in which the "even-tempered, good-looking" young man's antagonists would be his exceptionally beautiful wife and her lover.

It appears then, for all three of these novels, that the choice of a conflict and the characterization of the antagonists comprised the very first step of the story-building process. All of the other steps of the process – the improvisation of incidents and of secondary characters – came into being as consequences of these first, fundamental decisions. For just as the incidents are the stages of the conflict, so the secondary characters help – in one way or another – to make these stages unfold.

For example, the three supposed blind men in *Dr. No* serve no other purpose than to introduce the conflict, while minor characters like the young woman who slashes Quarrel's face and the thug who leaves a deadly centipede in Bond's hotel room are only fictional expedients for cranking up the danger. A host of characters in Austen's novel exist primarily to introduce and heighten conflict. Jane, because she is a sympathetic character and because Elizabeth loves her, is a major source of Elizabeth's conflict: Darcy's interference in Jane's romance is a wedge that keeps Elizabeth and Darcy apart. The function of the unsympathetic characters in *Pride and Prejudice* is also to introduce and increase conflict: Austen created Mrs. Bennet, Bingley's sisters, Lydia, Wickham and Lady Catherine in order to generate complications for her heroine. In *A Handful of Dust* Mrs. Beaver is a secondary character who first serves the purpose of introducing the conflict and later (by renting Brenda an apartment and then bringing her entourage of harpies to Tony's gothic castle) of making things worse and worse. Little John Andrew is another by-product of the structural requirements of the conflict: he exists solely for the purpose of dying in the middle of the book and so serving as a catalyst who precipitates the crisis. After Waugh invented Little John Andrew, the child's nurse and his horse-riding instructor, Ben, came into being as necessary adjuncts.

In *Pride and Prejudice* Darcy's cousin, Fitzwilliam, is another secondary character who apparently came into being in order to trigger a crucial turning point of the conflict: because it was necessary to make Elizabeth reject Darcy's proposal in the middle of the book, it was necessary first to have someone tell Elizabeth that Darcy had disrupted Jane's romance – and so Austen invented Fitzwilliam in order to convey this information.
The Gardiners, Elizabeth Bennet's worthy aunt and uncle, also exist as characters in order to serve the structural requirements of the unfolding conflict: their chief function in the novel is to initiate the process of bringing the conflict to a close. In *A Handful of Dust* Jock Grant-Menzies is yet another character created for the purpose of bringing about a crucial plot twist: for Jock appears to owe his fictional existence to Waugh's decision to conclude the marital conflict with a final irony -- – by rewarding Brenda with a new husband.

The antagonists actualize the conflict in flesh-and-blood. The way they are characterized – James Bond and Dr. No, Elizabeth and Darcy, Tony and Brenda – informs the design of each phase of their battle.

The secondary characters are the antagonists' satellites, who come into being in order both to elicit their personalities and to make the stages of their conflict unfold. In *Dr. No* James Bond's girlfriend, Honeychile Rider, performs both of these functions. Like other heroines in other Bond stories, she brings a facet of Bond's personality into view – his identity as a lover. But, at the same time, she plays a role in the stages of the central conflict. For example, she is the one who – by sailing her boat in plain view – provokes the attack by Dr. No's henchman. She also amplifies Bond's showdown with Dr. No by facing her own crisis at the same time. And, of course, she helps provide a coda to the conflict by joining Bond in one of Fleming's signature scenes of lovemaking.

Whereas James Bond's conflict with Dr. No is against an entirely external enemy, Elizabeth's and Darcy's battle is, at least partly, an internal one. They are both, in other words, self-divided antagonists -- waging internal conflicts while confronting one another. In order to dramatize Elizabeth Bennet's internal conflict – in order to call forth her prejudice, Austen invented the speciously attractive Wickham. And in order to dramatize Darcy's internal conflict – in order to objectify his pride, Austen conferred his false values on Lady Catherine de Bourg. Both of these secondary characters (Wickham and Lady Catherine) were invented in order to make the conflict between -- and within -- the antagonists unfold.

   Tony Last is another protagonist who is fighting two battles at the same time. On the one hand, of course, he is beset by an external conflict -- triggered by Brenda's affair with the odious John Beaver. But Tony is also his "own worst enemy." It is the external conflict, the breakdown of his marriage, that is most in evidence in the first and longer section of the novel, before Tony has gone off on his expedition in Brazil. But once he winds up in the jungle, Tony's asinine, self-destructive potential (the romanticizing blindness previously in the background of the first section of the book) at last takes center stage. In order to dramatize his protagonist's self-sabotage, Waugh had to invent the incidents and secondary characters of Tony's ordeal in the jungle before he falls into the clutches of the Dickens-loving Mr. Todd. For it is Tony's high-minded fantasy life that lures him into the rainforest – where, instead of a magical lost city, he discovers a succession of horrors.

   So characters who make problems for themselves – like Tony Last and Elizabeth Bennet – are brought to life in fiction by incidents that dramatize their misunderstandings and mistaken choices and by the secondary characters required to realize these incidents in flesh and blood. Elizabeth wins her battle with herself – finally seeing through the prejudices and mistaken judgments that Wickham, her negative alter ego, embodies. But Tony Last tops off his humiliating defeat by shooting himself in the foot. While Elizabeth Bennet learns from her conflict with herself, there is no reason to believe that Tony Last is any the wiser. Neither of them resembles James Bond, who remains as blissfully above doubt and misjudgment as he is impervious to change. And yet all three of them are brought to life by the ever-changing energy of evolving conflict. And so this conflict is essential for the novelist as well. Because it is conflict, like flint against steel, that gives the gift of fire.

About the Author

Terry Richard Bazes is the author of *Lizard World* (Livingston Press) and of *Goldsmith's Return* (White Pine Press). His personal essays and fiction have appeared in a number of publications, including *The Washington Post Book World, Newsday, Columbia Magazine, Travelers' Tales: Spain, Lost Magazine* and the *Evergreen Review*. He is a graduate of Columbia College and has a Ph.D. in English Literature from the State University of New York at Stony Brook. His doctoral dissertation, entitled *Romance and Realism in the Early Novel*, a study of the role of the fantastic in 17th- and 18th-century fiction, has served as a theoretical framework for his novels.

Praise for *Lizard World*:

"As the 18th century clashes with the 21st century by means of a kidnapping, an elixir of youth, an old manuscript, several murders, and many grisly incidents, a macabre tale unfolds that leaves everyone changed. The eccentric author of Goldsmith's Return presents a Florida gothic fable that both amuses and horrifies as its gruesome story takes shape. VERDICT: Readers fond of dark comedy and the macabre may get a kick out of this oddly compelling (and sometimes disturbingly graphic) tale."
—*Library Journal*

"A crazy, bawdy world of surrealist absurdities brought to life with a dazzling literary palette." -- *Shelf Awareness*

"Lurid and grotesque, this darkly comic tale revels in depravity and decadence; arcane knowledge leads to horror and ambition leads to destruction." -- *Publishers Weekly*

Praise for *Goldsmith's Return*:

"A novel of unusual ability and imagination." – Joseph Heller

"*Goldsmith's Return* is an impish tour de farce of dark humor, a bubbling cauldron of Pynchonesque paranoia, Dostoevskian humiliation, Kafkaesque body-loathing and punishing language a la Philip Roth, all simmered down to a thick, pungent, Gothic sauce." -- *The Buffalo News*

" A panoply of characters, from a dwarf artist to an obese, new-age cowgirl with ESP named Dagmar, recall the work of John Irving in their uncanny provision of a bizarre, yet oddly accurate, reflection of life." -- *The San Francisco Review of Books*

www.ingramcontent.com/pod-product-compliance
Ingram Content Group UK Ltd.
Pitfield, Milton Keynes, MK11 3LW, UK
UKHW041305180426
11947UKWH00009B/707